POEMED

POEMED

By Charles Wayne Cumbie

Publisher: Cumbie & Sons Press

This is a work of fiction, but often reflects events or interpretations of life as seen through the eyes of the author.

Text Copyright © 2019 by Charles Wayne Cumbie

Jacket Copyright @ 2019 by Michael W Cumbie

All rights reserved. Published in the United States by Cumbie & Sons Press

ISBN 978-1-7339014-0-6 (Hardback)

Book Design by Michael W Cumbie

Art images were downloaded from publicdomainvectors.org, and are bound to Creative Commons Deed CC0

Printed in the United States of America

First Edition

For my wife, who always thanks me for being brave enough to have had six children with her, when the truth is, it was her love that gave me the courage.

TABLE OF CONTENTS

PREFACE i

INTRODUCTION 1

FAMILY 2

    Ode to Debbie my Wife of 27 years With Love from Wayne (Anniversary) 2

    Cherish the Moment 3

    The Pledge, I Stand by You 4

    Birthday 5

    Hello Mom, I Miss You 6

    Goodbye Pete, My Brother 7

    What Comes Naturally 8

    Chester (Epitaph) 9

    Kayla Epitaph 9

    Kayla's Song 10

    Love's Glow 11

    To Dream of Sleep and Sleep to Dream 12

    Happy Birthday Brendan 13

    A Traveler's Poem 14

    Four Winds 15

    Remember (Your Children's Song) 16

    Wedding Poem for Andrew and Kathy 17

For Sarah My Daughter	18
Ode to a Pet	19
Earth Wife	20
Coming Home	21
Fly too Far	22
Friend of Mine	23
A Happy Birthday to All	24
Byron's Name Sake	24
Love Coming Down, Love All Around	25
The Birth of a Family	26
Spun Fun	27
The Three Sillies	27
Ballerinas	28
Angel Face	29
Come Home	30
Fairy House	32
A Note for Debbie's Birthday	34
A Toast	34
Reminisce	36
Amelia	37
Family Bond	38
Beautiful Child	39
HOLIDAY	42

Fall of the Innocent 42

Happy Easter 43

Harvest Time... 44

Christmas Tree Gift 45

Christmas Time 46

Christmas Upon Us 47

Happy Christmas 48

It's Christmas Time 48

LOVE 50

Let's Go 50

Song of My Life 52

Lonely Place 53

Silence is Not Golden.. 54

For Debbie With Love (Valentine) 54

Get Well.. 55

My Valentine Wishes for You "Pooh".............................. 56

Another Silly Love Poem 56

... ay Poem 57

A Bit of Time 58

Precious.. 59

Love Sick for You 60

Enough (First Valentine) 61

Be Mine Valentine 61

What Can I Buy?	62
Beauty and the Rest	63
Before You	64
Better than Most	66
My Last Will and Testament Valentine	67
Hand-in-Hand	67
Yes	68
Love at First Sight	70
Desert Rose	71
By Her, the Future	72
Longing for the Loss	74
If You Were My Valentine	76
Love'n You Brown Eyes	78
Emerald Green	79
Shadowy Eyes	80
Honey Bee No Memory	81
I Met a Girl and it Made All the Difference	82
If Beauty had a Name	84
Dear One	86
New Born	87
When You are Close to Me	88
Love	89
Pursuit of Dreams	90

Beauty 91

Still Mine 92

Fate Turns 93

Love Sick... 94

Dear Valentine 95

Love's Token 96

Sweet, Sweet Jane.. 96

Into the Sun 98

Beautiful Memories... 99

Grace 100

43 Years Young 101

Goodbye My Love 102

Small Valentine Poem... 103

44 Years 104

Lonely Soul (Can you hear the Echo?) 105

OTHER.. 106

The Family Pet... 106

Nothing.. 110

What Color Do I Paint My Jet?...................................... 110

Just Hit'em.. 112

Hurray for the Losers 113

Never Give Up 114

Song of Life.. 116

Taylor Swift 117

Such A Little Thing 118

Jackie Marie Evancho..119

Comfy Nest 120

Inventor 121

Tee it Up 122

Small Beach Poem..123

The Master Eraser 124

A Dollar for the Plate...126

Thoughts for a Skier 127

When the Seagulls Walk 128

A Beautiful Day..130

In 1989 Country Went Pop..132

Now I Know the Art of Memory...................................133

Sweet Madness 134

Fast Food..135

Computer Vs Books...136

Knight's Eye..138

The Black Box...140

Plan B..142

Seasoning 144

Inspiring Tale of Grace 145

Boondocking (A Poem of Freedom)..........................146

OLD AGE 148

One Last Time 148

Goodbye.. 148

Silver Hair 149

Have to Go 150

The Long Shadow.. 150

Waking Up 151

Last.. 152

Good Bye 152

Final Goodbye... 153

Travel Bag of Life 154

Old, So Old 155

The Box 156

Sad Eyes 157

Tired and Retired 157

Free and Retired... 158

So It's Your Birthday 159

The Misty Mist 160

Bone Garden 162

Vision Eyes 163

Bluesy 164

The Old Man 165

Cold 166

Shady Ghost 167

Free at Last 168

As I Go By, I Pass Away 169

Masterful Illusion 170

Slow-Mo 171

Enjoying God's Retirement Plan 172

The Countdown 173

So, It's Your Birthday Version 2 174

Downstream 175

Will It Be 176

Retired 177

Shake Rattle and Roll 178

Uphill Both Ways 179

On the Street (Another Box Poem) 180

Epitaph 181

The Four Horsemen 182

The Complaint 184

Cremation Blend 184

POETRY 186

Instructions 186

What's a Poem? 186

Why Bother 186

Poetry of a Song 187

A Rhyme in Time (A Poet's Lament) 188

The One Liner 189

Poets' Poem 190

The Poet 192

The Poet Part Two 193

If there is no Ear to Hear 194

Poetic Thoughts 194

Death of a Poem 195

Beautiful Words 196

Write On 197

POLITICS 198

The Plight of the Butterflies 198

Weep for the Future 199

Capitalism at Its Best 200

Needy Poor 202

The Flower 203

Arlington 204

Declaration 206

RELIGION 208

Nothing Left to Give 208

Answer to a Prayer 208

The Righteous Path 210

Secret Place 210

Gently the Soft Fall	211
After Life (Son Rise)	212
Beyond Measure	212
Judgement	213
You Know Not	214
Forgive Us	215
Don't Care Anymore	216
Signs of the Times	218
Jumping in the Volcano	220
The Apology	221
Silent Prayer	222
Silent Prayer (Short Version)	223
He's in the Book (of Life)	224
When Rocks and Stones Begin to Sing	225
The Righteous Rich	226
God's Conversation with an Inventor	228
Looking Up	229
Heaven's Gate	230
The Ohmn of the Didge	231
A Better Way	232
Will God Make it Right	233
Care of the World	234
Can God be Surprised?	235

Worship	236
God's People	237
A Prayer	238
Dawn (The Watcher)	240
God Among Us	241
Getting High	242
A Bridge to Nowhere	243
Kindness is the First Fruit	243
Ghost	244
They Prayed	245
God's Witness/Choose a Gift	246
You Only Have to Believe	247
In God We Trust	248
A Promise Given	250
To Plead	251
Tough Love	252
Evolution Solution	254
Choose Wisely	256
After Life (The Question)	257
For the Love of God	258
A Simple Thought	260
Death's Sting	262
Oh! God Where Are You?	264

    Happily Ever After 265

    Ode to My Lord 266

REFLECTIONS... 268

    Echoes of the Past 268

    Too Much 268

    I Name You 269

    Calm 270

    Dead Thoughts 271

    The Lost and Found 272

    Despair 273

    To Cry Alone 274

    The Other Side of Town 275

    Together Again 275

    Spring... 276

    Some of Me (Sorry for the Bragg) 278

    A Spring Day Walk.. 279

    The Boy and the Kite 280

    Just A Soul 282

    Wagon Maker.. 283

    The Pool.. 284

    Luck is all you got 286

    What Ya Gonna Do 286

    Hello.. 288

The Caeser Coin 290

Bury your Dead 292

A Stranger's Pen 293

Sounds 294

Stories Told 295

ACKNOWLEDGEMENTS 296

ABOUT THE AUTHOR 297

PREFACE

I started writing poems when I was 51 years old. My initial inspiration came from Lincoln's Gettysburg Address. It was so impressive and so moving that I thought it would be interesting to parody the address with the subject matter changed to family instead of soldiers. So, this parody of Lincoln's Gettysburg Address became my first poem.

It started me on my poemed journey. I wrote it for my wife Deborah on the 15th of June 2001, our 27th wedding anniversary. I liked the way it turned out and I have been trying to write interesting poems ever since. I invite you to come with me now as I wander my way through the streets of the poetic world. Who knows maybe you too, will become poemed.

INTRODUCTION

Hello to my dearest friends and family and to any other curious readers who may find themselves caught between my pages. My name is Charles Wayne Cumbie-- my mother always called me Wayne, so Wayne it is. This is my book of poems and I hope you find them interesting, thought provoking, and fun. They are best read by candle light, but barring that, any light will do. They have no expiration date except for that of mortal memory. In them you will find my poet's heart and an attempt to rhyme every time.

FAMILY

Ode to Debbie my Wife of 27 years With Love from Wayne (Anniversary)

Written: June 15th, 2001
About: Adapted from Lincoln's Gettysburg address

Two score and seven years ago this couple brought forth a union conceived of love and dedicated to the proposition that each were equal.

Now, they are engaged in a great struggle in the winter of life, not knowing whether their aging health would hold against the demands of time.

They were wed on this great battlefield of life, testing whether their family or any family so conceived and so dedicated could long endure, and have given 27 years of their lives, so that this family might live and prosper.

And, so from this honored couple we may take increased dedication to that cause for which they have given their full measure of devotion.

That the children of their union will here highly resolve that this mother and father will have not struggled in vain, and that their family, under God, shall have new birth and that this family, of the children and by the children, and for the children shall not perish from the Earth.

CHARLES WAYNE CUMBIE

Cherish the Moment

Written: August, 2010
Dedication: To Sarah
About: A time when Sarah was his Christmas child

The father looked in on his sleeping young daughter, knowing her 12th Christmas day would soon be upon her. A tender age that was just right for a Christmas filled with excitement and delight. For a little while he watched her as she slept through the night; and the father, usually so busy with the affairs of life, stood still and cherished the sight, wanting to always remember her in this light. He stilled his mind and warmed his soul as he watched his beautiful child sleeping through this Christmas Eve night.

The Pledge, I Stand by You

Written: August 27th, 2010

When comes the time
To hold that line
And there's no more give and take
All that's left is make or break
I stand by you

I share life's cost
Though all seems lost
I see it through and
I stand by you

And when it's tough to stay around
I hold my ground
Without fear or frown
I stand by you

As long as there's breath to stay awake
Never will you, I forsake
The strength of my arm is yours to take
I stand by you

Birthday

Written: October, 2010

As the years tic-toc themselves away
It is the birthday that starts the clock
Every year it marks the spot
Oh, what a happy day
For it all started for you this day
And, may the happiness from that event
Follow you through all your days
So, please let me give to you this helpful hint
It's friends and family along the way
That makes the days go well spent
So, eat the cake and ice cream too
But make no mistake that this is true
It's the smiles of friends and family
That are the icing on the cake.

Hello Mom, I Miss You

Hello Mom, I miss you, you know
I see us there walking side by side going home
You were alone and so was I but you were always there
You were the one who always cared
You never left me
Even though together we stood alone
You made sure I always had a place to be going home
Even though that time has come and gone
And I've lost you and that little boy
Still I see us there, it's etched in my mind
We were mother and son, walking side by side
In the warm summer sunshine going home
How I long to bring back that day
But it's a time that is long gone
Of mother and son walking home

CHARLES WAYNE CUMBIE

Goodbye Pete, My Brother

Written: April, 2011

Oh, my brother, this is our saddest day
The day you must release the spirit
And cross over where a new world awaits

It's good there, they say
A new body with no pain
And all your old mates to greet you again
The last good old boy has come home

And, may you give a helping hand
On that day that I can no longer stand
In this world and must cross over
To see the good old boys
And meet you again my brother

What Comes Naturally

Written: June 3, 2011

Once my house was full of family
Now they're grown and I'm left alone in this empty home
I guess that's just what comes naturally

Sometimes they come by to say 'Hi'
But then there's still that…. good bye
I know that it has to be this… a way
I guess that's just what comes naturally

If I had a rhyme or reason, I'd change it back
And hold my family near to me
But, I know I must yield to
What comes naturally

So, I'll just set here and dust off
My finest memories of a family that
Was dear to me

And, you know that's just
What comes naturally

Chester (Epitaph)

Written: October 20, 2011

I knew you at your finest hour
When you caught mice lighting fast
I knew you at your saddest hour
When death's claws began slowly to sink in
And, I said goodbye to you
With each toss of the shovel's dirt
I hope you have found your way from this ground to a
place of no suffering or hurt

Kayla Epitaph

Written: May 21, 2011
Dedication: For Kayla our cat who died 21 May 2011, a Saturday night; she lay down in the tall grass of our backyard and went to sleep. I buried her on that spot that she had chosen.

When I lay me down for that big sleep
Give to me no flaming Viking ship
For I would rather have to keep
Just a mouse between my paws to nip

Kayla's Song

Written: May 23, 2011
Dedication: A Blues Song for my Cat Kayla

Kayla, Kayla where are you today
I went and called your name
But there was silence from your grave
Kayla, Kayla where are you today
We've been friends for 13 years along life's way
Now it's with tears that I must pay
Kayla, Kayla where are you today
I'm afraid I'll never again see you play
I reach out my hand, but I must understand
That you can't come to me again
Oh, Kayla Kayla, where are you today
I need a friend, but you've passed away
Oh, Kayla Kayla are you aware of that promise made
We'll meet again on that fine day
When the son bids rise to those that lay

CHARLES WAYNE CUMBIE

Love's Glow

Written: August 23, 2011 at 3am
Dedication: For my daughter-in-law, Melissa

Your life within will soon be your own
With life born anew, your days will be brighter too
A trio of fun with parties in the sun
A new family for the world to welcome in
A mother's care, and a father's watch
Keeps safe this child so fair
Held close to the breast, while she rests
Behold, Love's glow of a mother's tenderness
As she holds her child close
And feels the young breath on her face
No dearer love can be found
Among the human race

To Dream of Sleep and Sleep to Dream

Written: May 26, 2012
Dedication: This poem is dedicated to my grandson, Brendan, who at four months is sleepless in Albany Oregon

As the day grows long
And I begin to yawn
Sing to me that sweet song
A lullaby to send me on
To my dream filled journey
Until the night becomes dawn
But if I wake to see the moon
Then I have awoke much too soon
So sing to me once again
That sweet song and send
Me back where I will stay
Till that golden sky beckons me
Rise to welcome the day

Happy Birthday Brendan

Written: January 22, 2013
Dedication: To my grandson, Brendan

So, Brendan
One year ago
The sun began to shine
For you for the first time
And now we celebrate that
Day for you with cake and cream
A son like you, a parent's dream
May your years be many
And the happy times plenty
Enjoy the cake and your time in the sun
As your mom and dad watch each
Birthday's growth and smile at your fun

A Traveler's Poem

Written: March 3, 2013
About: Written for Andrew when he was flying away from home

The wayward visitors on their way
No time to play or smell the roses as they say
They know the road ahead is long
Still they take that first step with a song
Soon they will be stuck between here and there
A traveler's nowhere
With hope sent up as a prayer
That they are safe from here to there
May their travels not be so long
That they run out of song
With a sad sigh
They are watched
As they slowly become smaller and smaller
Until they are gone
A father's goodbye
As they are watched
With sad eye

CHARLES WAYNE CUMBIE

Four Winds

Written: June 18, 2013

I know you must go
As the four winds blow
But whether you face
North, south, east, or west
Know that you are loved
And are wished all the best
Though your sun will now set
At a different time
You will still be always
On our mind
May God's grace shine
Down around you and settle
Like the warmth from the
Touch of a kind and caring hand
till the happiness you seek
Finds you at peace

Remember (Your Children's Song)

Written: July 5, 2013

Do you remember the sun on your face
Our moment, happiness to embrace
When life meant only to be with you
Near you, close to you
The fun was from sun to sun
Children laughing in the yard
Playing games of make believe
Practicing on the future feats they will achieve
No worries to care, polish, or shine
Too busy having fun in the sunshine
No need to worry what you eat
Health given as freely as the breeze in the trees
A body that was easy to move, dance, and enjoy
Life was like an elaborate toy
Drank from a cup till the last drop has you looking up
May you remember loves moments and sweet kisses
And listen to your children's' song
Until their echoes are gone

CHARLES WAYNE CUMBIE

Wedding Poem for Andrew and Kathy

*Written: July 28, 2013 * [Expanded Feb 17 2014]*
About: To my son Andrew, and his wife Kathy

Now the wedding bells have chimed for you
And with your yes, you both set out on a heavenly quest
[This path you take together
Has the promise of forever
May kindness be your guide
As you hold your course side by side]
And may your love carry you through
All the wrong that the world can do
Carry you over any troubled sea
And may you be guided by the light you adore
To a safe and pleasant shore

For Sarah My Daughter

Written: August 20, 2013
Dedicated: To Sarah

I miss you, all the cheerful happy things you do
When you took your children and left a vacant house
You left me with a vacant heart

Now, I wonder when the loneliness
Like a heavy wet fog that settles in
Will ever lift so I can see you again

But, I can't complain if you're not here
To hear me call your name
Or to see the gift of your smile
For, you were ours for awhile

And, now it's time to give you up
For the clock of destiny has struck
So far away you must go
And with love I wish you luck
With the new life that you now sew

CHARLES WAYNE CUMBIE

Ode to a Pet

Written: February 9, 2014
Dedication: For Kayla

When you chose your spot
To settle in to wait for the end
You looked at me with eyes of goodbye
You know I'll keep that memory close within
I didn't know that your last sleep
Would last forever
And that you would never
See the day's dawn
And from my life you would be gone
I was the only one who noticed
That you had chosen your way out
So, I knew where to look when
You didn't come out
You had to drink from the cup
That God's given
Even the Son had to stop living
Where you are, may your days
Be lazy and dreamy
Warming in the sun
Still playful, still having fun

Earth Wife

Written: March, 2014

With my last breath
I whisper your name
With my last thoughts
In the sky I write your name
Yours will be my last embrace
As I gaze the last time upon your face
The withering has come
And sunken in body I am
But there is hope offered
By the purchase of the Lamb
And though I turn my face to the east
I see the sun not rising, it's setting
Even so, I know
I may still be invited to the feast
So, goodbye my love
My Earth wife
Though in the Earth I'm lain
May we meet again
In another life
And walk hand in hand into
That celestial light
On a higher plane

CHARLES WAYNE CUMBIE

Coming Home

Written: March 12, 2014

Coming home
The first contact comes from
Far away on the phone
And, you know that soon
You won't be alone
The visit is long awaited
From a distance fated
The house is made ready
The clock holds steady
You can't make it go faster
As you hope there's no disaster
You can't wait to invite them in
And ask them how they've been
You will ask the usual questions
Of travel and time
But the most important one
Is are you fine
I watch through the window
And up the road
To be sure I'm there to help you unload
And, as the smiles are passed around
Like a handshake given
It's these kinds of happy times
That makes life worth liven

Fly too Far

Written: March 29, 2014

When the bird flies too far to hear her song
Too far to touch, she is gone
Gone as gone as can be
Her song now echoes in another world
Under another sun and moon
And you miss that happy tune
It is too far to touch
Gone as gone as can be
And though you call out
With all your breath
She is too far to touch
Gone as gone as death
It may be that when the
Shadow of your life grows long
Only then will you hear again
The happy tune of her song
Under a new sun and new moon
May the eye and ear be blessed soon

CHARLES WAYNE CUMBIE

Friend of Mine

Written: April 16, 2014
Dedication: For Sophie, man's best friend

I removed the collar
From your neck
Cause I know you'll be
Running free
Where you go next
One shot to the dark
One more to go home
I stayed with you
So, you weren't alone
You had to leave us
Without even a stone
Now, close to my heart
You live on
You still take your
Place next to me
Always there in memory
You will always be
My Sophie

p.s. Sophie, our dog and friend for 15 years died on this day

A Happy Birthday to All

Written: June 29, 2014
Dedication: For Andrew

Happy birthday to those that play
Happy birthday to those who think it's just another day
Happy birthday to those who don't have the time of day
Happy birthday to those who would use their wish to wish it away
I say happy birthday to us all
The happy birthday it's the only day of the three-sixty-five
That shows you're still alive
So happy birthday to all those who will come out to play
And happy birthday to you Andrew, my son
And one by one may all your dreams be won

Byron's Name Sake

Written: July 16, 2014
Dedication: To my grandson, Byron

Byron, did you know
You have a name sake
He was a champion of golf
May in life your aim be as straight
And that you always rise
Above all you undertake
You started the race a little small
But soon you will catch them all

CHARLES WAYNE CUMBIE

Love Coming Down, Love All Around

Written: June 23, 2014

Like manna coming down
My family circles round
Cheering me on to rise up
From that killing ground
To face my fate
And one more time, fight another round
I did not think I had it in me
But I draw strength from my loving family
They cheer me on with their energy
My age has set me on the exit stage
My future like a dying ember
But my family gathering round
Fans the living ember
So, I rise and stumble on
Though my strength is almost gone
But, for their love I carry on

p.s. Thank you, Andrew and Kathy, for the Father's Day card and gift. Your thoughtful kindness inspired this poem.

The Birth of a Family

Written: July 17, 2014

Dedication: To my grandchild Charlie, born to Kathy and Andrew

Unto you a child is born
And with the light in his eyes
A family is born
You both will see a child's world again
Full of excitement and fun and happy endings
Birthdays and Christmas, Easter and
Campouts and summer fun
School days of ABC's and how to spell his name
Pictures taken of those first steps
A scrap book of remembrance kept
To mark his glory days
Clothes that are frightfully small
But don't worry for all
Too soon he will grow tall
And as the sun shines on your child's face
To keep up you will have to race
For he with his youthful energy will set the pace
And your days will be the fullest of all
For the gift he brings is the best of all
The happy endings

CHARLES WAYNE CUMBIE

Spun Fun

Written: August, 2014
Dedication: For Maddy, my granddaughter

There was a girl
Who loved to twirl
She would spin round and round
Till she fell down
Laughing as she watched
The world spin round
Her brother and sisters
Thought it quite funny
And would join in the fun
So, they all spun
Round and round
Till laughing they all
Fell to the ground
May you always have such joy
That you laugh till you fall down

The Three Sillies

Written: March 4, 2016
About: A poem by Tabitha, Maddy, and Grandpa

Three silly magicians
Played silly tricks
And they accidentally
Turned themselves
Into a bundle of sticks

Ballerinas

Written: 2015
Dedication: For Tabitha, my granddaughter

Once there was a girl named Tabbalina
Who had a sister named Maddadreama
They both liked to play and dance like a ballerina
One day Tabbalina began to spin so fast
That she spun clean out of sight
And everyone began to ask
'Have you seen Tabbalina?'
Maddadreama missed her sister and was so sad
But Tabbalina only spun for fun
And she came back again that night
When Maddadreama saw Tabbalina
She was so happy and glad
That they played and laughed
Until they could play no more
And the next day they were both
Tabbalina and Maddadreama
So very very sore

Angel Face

Written: May 23, 2015
Dedication: For Kathy and Andrew's baby Charlie

Sweet little baby
You're such a happy guy
You're giving me your sleepy eye
So, I don't think you'll need a lullaby
But, maybe if I sing soft enough
I can still hear you sigh
As you relax into your angle face
And in your crib with comfy
Blanket will be placed

Come Home

Written: June 4th, 2015
About: Written for my daughter, Sarah

My Gypsy Family

Come home
Come home to me
My lovely gypsy family
The ache is real
The longing deep
Your happy smiles are what I need

Come home
Come home to me
My lost and distant family
And with you near I know I'll feel
The mending of my heart
That my tears have failed to heal

Come home
Come home to me
My far away family
For I have flung open my door
And eagerly wait to see
Your happy faces once more

CHARLES WAYNE CUMBIE

Come home
Come home to me
My young family
And may god honor the blessing I give
That your journey be safe and sound
'Til your travels are done
And once more at home be found

POEMED | FAMILY

Fairy House

Written: March 16, 2016
About: Inspired by my granddaughter Tabitha's imagination

One day I built a fairy house
It was tiny, as was their way
Made of sticks encircled bound
In shape of pointy hat upon the ground
Its floor leafed of nature's green
So, they, if ventured there could
Softly settle down
Alas, forlorn was my day
For they did not come out to play
So, I thought to entice with sweet
Nectar drink, and cookie dough
And wait I did, to see if this would
Be enough to summon them to show
Alas, again my day forlorn, no visit
Was made on fairy silent wing
But to my surprise, my wait was no more
When the loud buzzing working bee
Showed up at the door
Still I waited till busy bee
And sunlight were gone
And as my little fairy house grew dark
It wasn't that way for long

CHARLES WAYNE CUMBIE

For firelight came to brighten my
Little fairy house, as the fireflies inside
Danced their game of on and off
So, maybe, just maybe, this was what it took
To summon the fairies near
And though they still hid too well to see
I could hear their fairy song
Serenading me

The fairy house that Tabitha made

A Note for Debbie's Birthday

Written: April 16, 2016
Dedication: For my wife, Debbie

So, it's another birthday
And you think old is 67
But there's no need for whining
There is a silver lining
For each birthday candlelight
Brings you closer to heaven
And as you wish, and wish you might
That the path to heaven be lit
By birthday candlelight

A Toast

Written: June 23, 2016
Dedicated: A poem for our college student Andrew Cumbie. Go forth and conquer the world.

A toast to the college years
And GPA fears
With knowledge overwhelming
We'll raise our glasses
To let all know that we will keep singing
Even through the tough classes
With cheery family to help stay strong

CHARLES WAYNE CUMBIE

As academic years begin to feel too long
We can still raise our glass and break out in song
Till the square hat is thrown
And with diploma in hand
We will sing with the band
To a new beginning

p.s.
Hi, Andrew and Kathy and Charlie. I'm writing you to thank you for the Father's Day card and the check you sent me. I will use the money to buy a nice meal or two, thanks again. I thought I'd send you a poem I wrote in the tradition of Edgar Allan Poe. He was said to have, after becoming well known, written small poems for payment of his meals and drink. So, I thought it would be fun to pay you for my food and drink with a poem written for you, addressing your college years. I hope this letter finds you all doing well. It will be fun to see you, Kathy and Charlie, in a few weeks for our yurt camp out. May your flight be safe and easy as you come home to us. You will be able to use David's car as much as you want while you are here. And, Laura has said you can stay at her house while you're here. Let's try to get as much fun in as we can. I'm sure you need a break from all that hard studying. So, we'll see you soon. Can't wait to see how much Charlies grown.

Yours,
Wayne Cumbie

Reminisce

Written: June, 2014
About: Prayer for the dead

Mom, Dad, Pete
Are you young again?
Are you happy?
Do you have fun things to do?
Is your labor a joy?
Virgie, Daulphus, Truely and Sadie
Early, and Sylvia, and Nathan
Are you young again?
Are you happy?
Chubby, Sophie, Chester
Mousie, and Kayla
Are you young again?
Are you happy?
Giving chase in the sun
Your shadows prancing
May the God that made us
Have the power to save us
And keep all his creation
Safe under his wing

Amelia

Written: July 7, 2016

About: For my granddaughter Amelia, may you fly as high as the sky

Hi, Amelia
I'm your grandfather
And I'm here to tell ya
You are the cutest little thing
Come down to walk with us
Without your wings
Newly unwrapped with God's gift of life
You are such a delightful sight
May you find here the love you need
And may all your choices to happiness lead
So, feel the warmth and comfort
Of your mother and father's arms
They will always protect you and
Keep you from harm
And, I from a distance will
Admire your progress
As you become a most beautiful princess

Family Bond

Written: March 22, 2017

When your light arrives
Sinking down from the skies
A new happier day is born
I greet you with the care of a father for his son
Happy that you're here
That you're near
You bring to me your family to see
A wife, a mother, and a happy playing child
Such a delight to see
I can feel the strength, the love of the family bond
And like a seer I can see beyond
To a future full of happy times
A family's nurture, smiles that shine
So keep on holding on to that family bond
For it's a powerful forging merciful love
It's stronger than any elemental bond
And the weight of the world will break against it
Yours will be an eternal legacy
With stars spelling out your family name
A family bond with the warmth of an eternal flame

CHARLES WAYNE CUMBIE

Beautiful Child

Written: December 28, 2018
Dedication: For my granddaughter Amelia

Amelia with her corn silk hair
So, fair
Plays all day without a care
With a smile that brightens the day
Then off again she goes to play
Who can say what she may be
Let's hope that whatever it be
That it lets her always be free
As free as the fairies of the wood
And as beautiful as the meadow flower
Open to the summer sun
So, play on my fair one
Have lots and lots of fun

The Cumbie Family: My wife, six kids, and I

CHARLES WAYNE CUMBIE

The Cumbie Family: My parents, brother, and I

HOLIDAY

Fall of the Innocent

Written: November 2010
About: Original version and alternate ending

He did not understand at all
He had caused no trouble
His family cringed against the wall
As strong arms dragged him from their midst
His feet tied and hobbled
He would be slain to spare the rest
His would be a martyr's test
Now, the sharpened ax had offed his head
And the innocent one was cleanly bled
Soon, with oven fired, all would be fed
For the Turkey that caused no trouble
Had lost his gobble
And was brought to his final rest
Spread piece by tasty piece
On the plates of the dinner guests

CHARLES WAYNE CUMBIE

Happy Easter

Written: April, 2011

When the Easter Bunny comes to town
All the kids run round and round
Looking for the sweetest eggs
Hard to find hidden on the ground
But once the fetching job is done
All that's left is the delicious fun

Harvest Time

Written: November 10, 2014

We raise our cups
To the workers of the fields
Who bring in the harvest
Good food, lined up
Juicy meats and pies so sweet
With a mouthwatering smell
Fond dishes we know so well
Family gathered
Happy laughter
It's a Thanksgiving holiday meal
With a southern comfort
Kick your shoes off kind of feel
It's a real fun time
As we enjoy and dine
Celebrating the year's harvest
Basking in the smiles of good company
Surrounded by all the love of family
Happy, happy Thanksgiving
And may all share in
The harvest that's been given

CHARLES WAYNE CUMBIE

Christmas Tree Gift

Written: December 9, 2014

Oh, Christmas tree
Tree of life
You are forever, evergreen
You bring each year
The Christmas cheer
Drawing together our
Loved ones dear
You sparkle and shine
Your lights to remind
Us all to be kind
For we all belong
To the family of mankind
Though below your branches
The gifts do lie
It's your crowning star
That reminds us why
For it was a star that lit the night
For, the child that was given,
Brings the greatest gift from heaven
A Christmas gift to all
A child born to save us from the fall
Who will one day say rise
And a new Christmas day will be born
Lit bright by the star of
an eternal morn

Christmas Time

Written: December 14, 2014

It's Christmas time
And the weather is wintry fine
All white and pristine clean
Let's make some snow ice cream
Put together our best snowman ever
Playing out in the weather
Breathe in the crisp winter air
Sing the holiday jingles with a flair
Maybe catch a ride on a slide
Try to make snow angels fly
Then me and you could make
A snowball or two
And when the night falls
And there's no more sun
We can still have fun
We'll watch the cheerful lights color the night
And go inside to get ourselves dry
By the warm fireside
Have a cup of chocolate
With marshmallow cream
Talk about the fun we've had
Sharing our time together
And how we'll do it again on the morrow

Watching for the snowflakes to fall
As we sink knee deep in the snow
Laughing and joking, having a ball

Christmas Upon Us

Written: December 20, 2014

Christmas is upon us
The sky filled with snow
Ready to put on a show
The smiles of the people
Following you around
Happy, happy are the sights and sounds
As they go shopping throughout the town
Carrying packages up to the chin
Children all excited for the fun to begin
Yes! The Christmas time is near
It's been a long wait
A whole year
Now all our dear ones have gathered near
And we all give a toast
To good cheer

Happy Christmas

Written: 2015

Christmas lights twinkling
Snow a falling
People, happy cheering
Saint Nick, ho, ho-ing
Reindeer towing
Loved ones' smiles showing
Laughter echoing
It's a time for caring
And a time for sharing
May all the unwrapping
Reveal the seasons meaning
Of spreading the joy
Of the Christmas giving
So, have a merry, merry Christmas
And may your joy be fulfilling

It's Christmas Time

Written: December 24, 2018

Ho! Ho! Christmas is here
Warm up the reindeer
Throw the magic dust
Get them in the air
Rudolf has his red nose

CHARLES WAYNE CUMBIE

And when he's happy it glows
You know he's happy when
Christmas is upon us
So, throw the magic dust
There's no waiting for a bus
We'll be here and there and Everywhere
In the twinkling of an eye
Over the rooftops we will fly
Bringing toys for boys and girls
But if you've been naughty and not nice
You might just get the old cold
Dust stocking surprise
So, be good and keep those eyes shut
'Cause I knows when you're awake
If you stay awake too long
It might just make me late
And I'm sure you don't want a no show
Ho! Ho!

LOVE

Let's Go

About: Compilation of notes

Let's go and we'll pick a dream to share
And try to spend our lives in the sun without a care
Let's go and find a piece of beach to make our own
And when we're done with our fun in the sun
Let's go and find a place with our favorite food
And we'll talk about dreams and plan a scheme
To make them all come true
Let's go, we'll hide out in a lover's cove
And I'll admire you and desire you
By the light of a lover's moon
Let's go together and we might find how wonderful our life can be
Let's go and see if there's a plan
That we can find where I'll be yours
And you'll be mine
Let's go, come with me
And I'll be your man, cause you're so pretty
I can't help but offer you my hand
No riches required, just your bubbly self is all I need
Let's go invite guests

CHARLES WAYNE CUMBIE

And throw a party
To show the rest of the world our love
Let's go and choose the path that
Will lead us to the starlight
And make our love glow so bright
That it lights up our life
Let's go and find a place
That is just ours and ours alone
And we'll remember it all of our lives
Let's go and find the place where our loved one's call home
And there we'll stay, no more need to roam

Song of My Life

As the life grows short
And the years grow long
I will always find a way
To sing for you
Because you are the song of my life
I will always long to be near to you
My wife, my light
And my heart will always sing for you
And to you I will always, always be true
I will always want to be your knight
And keep you safe in my arms through the night
You my wife, have saved my life
And for that I will always, always hold you so dear
And I know it's been a long time coming
But I want you to know here and now
That I love you and always will
For you are the song of my life
My love, my wife
How dear you are to me
My dear, loving wife
You are the song of my life
No matter where I go or what I do
My heart will always sing for you
And the wedding bells rung long ago
Still sound just as clear

For you are the one that's dear
You are the song of my life
Any time of day or month or year
I will always want you near

Lonely Place

You left me in a lonely place
You left me, dust in my face
It wasn't enough of a disgrace
You left me alone in a lonely place
One of these days we'll meet again
And once more I'll take it on the chin
My love for you won't let me win
And once again you'll be in the wind

Silence is Not Golden

Written: June 22nd, 2010
Dedication: For my wife Debbie of 36 years

I'm sorry, Debbie, that your world is growing silent.
What a sadness it must be to no longer hear the music or the breeze in the trees.
To miss the voices of your children and their children.
To not be able to know the thoughts of others, which their voices must convey.
I wish there was something I could do or say, to make this curse go away.
No longer can there be a whisper of sweet nothings or a witty joke to say.
But someday, in a distant future, there will be a brighter world and day.
And you will hear me call to you to please come out and play.

For Debbie With Love (Valentine)

Written: June 15th, 2009
Dedication: For my wife Debbie on Valentine's Day

Roses are red
Violets are blue
I said I do and you did too
Together, blazing a trail

Through the hazards of life
Looking back 35 years
Long out of sight
And through all the difficulties
That we've been through
The answer is still, and always, I do
For a promise is given unto you
That no one can undo, that I do
And when the trail ends
And the path is no more
I'll whisper your name, and reach
For your hand, and together we'll
Take one step more
Onto a new path into evermore
For a promise was given unto you
That no one can undo, that I do

Get Well

Written: January, 2011

Oh, my tender love
So sad that you feel bad
May you get better, but till then
Enjoy these gifts I send
I hope they cheer you up
And help you win your
Struggle to mend

My Valentine Wishes for You "Pooh"

Written: Summer, 2010
Dedication: To my wife, Debbie

May you always be able to find your way back to the green acre wood. Where I'll be your Christopher, and we'll spend our days exploring the paths in that gentle wood. Helping the noble Pooh and his friends to stay out of trouble again.

May you always stay the shiny eyed, little Seaside girl I've come to know, and never stray far from that 100 acre wood.

Another Silly Love Poem: Love Stays

Written: August, 2010

How do I love you, there are so many ways
You know this love I have for you will last through all my days
And though the nights may be cold or warm, still my love stays

And though my life be spring or winter, you will always be dear to me, for still my love stays

As the pages of our history are added to each day, still my love stays
And I could never leave you, no, there's just no way
For the pain of missing you would never go away
So, if I say I love you in so many ways
It's because this love I have for you is not a silly phase
And through all our days together, still my love stays

... ay Poem

Written: October 6th, 2010

When love comes to stay
There's nothing needed to say
Each day feels like a good day
Two souls unite in love's play
And creation takes notice as if to say
It knows that love's the eternal way
Brighter even than any sun's ray

A Bit of Time

Written: November, 2010
Dedication: For Debbie, my loving wife and travel companion

She was lovely in the sunlight
Orange pop and leather pants
The blue sky over her shoulder
How could I not long to hold her
A break from the promises of the road ahead
Two young people newly wed
A stop, a picture taken
To cement in place this bit of time
And, as they renewed their journey onward
Many more roads would they share
Now, the old man stands and stares
At this bit of time, so small
Yet so dear to recall
Then with tender care
Puts the picture back on the wall

CHARLES WAYNE CUMBIE

Precious

Written: January, 2011

In the pocket of my jeans
I have a precious thing
No gold can buy it
No skill can acquire it
Only, by God's gift can you come by it
It's a picture of us when you loved me
A love I know made the angels smile
Even though our love was only for awhile
It felt as if it was an eternity
All our fields were green
We let the young doves fly
And chased every frowning cloud from the sky
And when we had our final farewell
I kept this precious thing to remember you by
This picture of loves first hello
With no hint of ever a goodbye

Love Sick for You

Written: January, 2011

If there was a way
To hold a sunny day
To not let it get away
I would hold it for you
For on any sunny day
Your skin is set aglow
Eyes and face all ashine
Sun's halo in your hair
It's a God's gift to behold one so fair
God's masterpiece has dropped
My soul to its knees
And for you I'm eager to please
I am drunk with your beauty as if
I've had too much of a rare wine
And such beauty commands me
That I can't turn away
And, if there was a way
I still would not want to turn away
And if I could have my way
I would shower you with tender endearments
All the rest of my days

CHARLES WAYNE CUMBIE

Enough (First Valentine)

Written: February 2011

You are my love
There is nothing else
Nor needs to be, it is enough
With you I need not to be someone else
Or something more, for in your eyes I am enough
How can I not long to be with you, when it is enough, no need for more
For on that first day when I carried you across the threshold of our door
It was enough, no need for more

Be Mine Valentine

Written: February 14, 2011
Dedication: For Debbie my wife

Oh, please say you'll be my valentine
And together we'll find
A love that can't be lost
A love so rare, we'll pay any cost
And hand in hand we will walk
That quiet garden path, forever together
Sharing a dream that can stand any weather
For when our souls entwine
We will create our own time
Such a sweet, sweet valentine

What Can I Buy?

Written: June 3, 2011

What can I buy that will satisfy the debt I owe to you
For the 37 years of love and tenderness?

And if I could, I would paint for you
The bluest sky without a single cloud nearby
But, God has already colored his sky
Your favorite shade of blue
For God always favors his angels true

What can I do or say that would give honor to that day
When you chose me to stay?

I know it must have been God's hand
That guided me your way
So, what can I give that could possibly repay
The yes from your lips on that happy day
When I asked if I could stay?

But, I know that man's gold, would simply grow old
I need to give you something you can hold
Something that will last for eternities
So, I give to you my hand
The hand of a lifelong friend

Who will journey with you till the very end

And even when the sun has lost its shine
And is no longer to be found
I know that I will still have you to put my arms around

Beauty and the Rest

Written: March 28, 2011

God gave her golden haloed hair
And put the blue of the sky in her eye
And cherries on her lips
And the sun's glow to warm her skin
Such beauty has to be a sin
Such temptation is sure to win
And you know you will have to give in
And bow down to this beauty queen
To ask for a quest to serve her best
For there can be no rest for a heart
Taken and held to love's breast

Before You

Written: September 25, 2011

Before you
I stood alone
Watching the snow fall
Soft and silent in the night
So lovely the sight
Unshared a dish without spice

Before you
I stood alone
Feeling the deep longing
Of a heart whose beat
Echoes the emptiness
Alone, strangers rushing past
Without a glance

Before you
I stood alone
My life adrift
No light to guide me home
No bell to sound the way

Before you
I stood alone

CHARLES WAYNE CUMBIE

My dreams were of how to find you
Fate my only hope and compass
As I lie awake
Sleepless in the night

But, for you
No longer alone
Now life has meaning
A frame to hold its place
As the soft flakes of snow
Float gently down around us
I feel His grace
As we stand together
Enjoying the sight
Sharing the moment
So rich with spice

Better than Most

Written: June 15, 2012
Dedicated: For my wife, on our 38th wedding anniversary

As the ghosts of my memory
Whisper our history
One thought always comes to mind
"Better than most"

We've spent our lives investing in each other
Dreaming together, it was a time
"Better than most"

And as we walked hand in hand
On that treadmill of years
There were tears of sadness,
Tears of happiness
But they were tears shared
It was a time
"Better than most"

And if they deem to raise a glass
In toast to our life's union
May it be said when they speak
Of our love that it was
"Better than most"

p.s. Just think if you make it to 100 and I make it to 99, we can have 38 more years

CHARLES WAYNE CUMBIE

My Last Will and Testament Valentine

Written: February 14, 2013
Dedication: For Debbie, my life's love

I want you to have all of …
All of my love
My last days
My last goodbye
My last kiss
And my last heartbeat, felt for you my last and only love
And my last wish for you is that my love was enough

Hand-in-Hand

Written: April 4, 2013

I spent my days of youth with you
my friend and lover, mother too
Those days were way too few, but
we had the most fun in the sun
You and me forever, forever
Hand-in-hand we walked the sand
As waves came in then back out again
As our lives ebe away and the high tide is no more
You can rest a shore
There we'll be forever, forever more
We'll walk the sand as waves come in and out again
Always together, together
Hand-in-hand

Yes

Written: June 28, 2013

Remember when
You looked wonderful
With your hair in the wind

Remember when
We became more than
Just friends

Remember when you said
Your first yes
And the movie we saw
Began our life's quest

Remember when you said
Your second yes
And the future stretched out
Before us like a magical
Celestial quest
Knowing that now, we begin
To walk together to life's unknown end

Such a small word, yet so powerful
A yes to open up life's treasure chest

CHARLES WAYNE CUMBIE

And always will I long for your sweet yes
It lifts me up to try my very best

So, when the time comes
And I'm laid to rest
Life's echo for me will always be
The sound of your sweet celestial yes
That raises me up to try my very best

Love at First Sight

Written: September 10, 2013

Your beauty is beyond compare
It doesn't matter what you wear
Like the sirens song you draw me near
The shine of your eyes
Makes me realize
There's nothing I can do but turn and stare
But please don't smile
Because if you do
It will take awhile
Just to breathe again
You're so far above me
That there's no way you could love me
So, I have to watch you
Walk away as a friend
And as you go
The light around me seems to dim
While your siren's song
Draws my heart onto its rocky end

CHARLES WAYNE CUMBIE

Desert Rose

Written: November 3, 2013

My desert rose
You used to be
Now you're not here
For me to see
You bring me home
In memory
And of your loss
I'll never be free
I hope someday
There'll come a time
Where there's no border
That can confine
And with moistened eyes
That do shine
I'll once again
Say you are mine

p.s. Written for Kathy, my new daughter-in-law

By Her, the Future ...

Written: November 11, 2013

By the sparkle in her eyes
I knew I'd love her till the day I died
And on bended knee I'd make her my bride

By the gentleness of her kiss
I came to know what I had missed
She was the flower that gave the garden its dye

By the warmth of her caress
She held me to her breast
And I knew my soul had found its rest
There would be no other place I'd rather be
I was the one for her and she the one for me

By her love she worked the miracle of life
My loving wife gave to us a beautiful family
And now together we have a place to be

By the kindness of her soul
She drew from me a well of love
And for happiness I would thirst no more

CHARLES WAYNE CUMBIE

By the beauty of her soul, she taught me
How to walk that Jordan's path
And in God's certain future of this we are sure:
Together we'll embrace and feel the warmth of his grace
As we take our place standing on that distant shore

Longing for the Loss

Written: January 16, 2014

There's a heartache that comes each day
Because you are away
You gave me reason to smile
Now there's just too many miles
To find my way to you
But I reach out into that telescopic sky
And try to use the inner eye
To imagine you busying about with your life
Doing those endearing things that might
Bring happiness to those around
Once you were so close
I could hear you breathe
but now there's only a memory you leave
And a heartache that comes each day that you are away
Gentle I hold your memory like a fragile flower unwithered
Holding onto its beauty, keeping it close
Well-fed with tears of care

No need to turn the light on
The darkness suits me just fine
Cause now you're gone
And so is my heart's song
With every step you take

CHARLES WAYNE CUMBIE

You get farther away
Too far to hear my voice
Call for you to stay
I know I can't fix this loss that we have
A love gone that once was shared
And now the heart cannot be spared
So, don't turn the light on
The darkness suits me
For the sound of your echoing footsteps
Has darkened my soul
And now the silent darkness suits me

If You Were My Valentine

Written: February 1, 2014

If you were my valentine
I would carpet your path
With pink petals
And have the songbirds
Serenade my love for you

If you were my valentine
I would hold your hand
On a sunshine beach
As we walk barefoot
On the glistening sand

If you were my valentine
I would build the cottage
And thatch the roof
To keep you warm
And bring to you
All the love a man can give
For it's the light of your smile
That makes my life worthwhile

If you were my valentine
I would dive the deep

CHARLES WAYNE CUMBIE

For the richest pearl
To let you know
You are my girl
And climb the highest tree
For the sweetest fruit
To give to thee

If you were my valentine
From the hills I would
Shout out my love
And let the echoes
Confess it again and again
To the sky above
For there could be no better love
It's you and only you
That makes my heart
Soar like the dove

If you were my valentine
With the strength of our love
We would never part
For you are the
Goddess of my heart

Love'n You Brown Eyes

Written: April 9, 2014
About: Mash-up of Brown Eyes and Love'n You

Love or not to love
That is not the question
It comes at you like the
Glass door you thought was open
You see the one that is
The only one
You hope it's not a one-way street
And that your love comes back from
The one you meet
When they breathe out
You want to breath in
And when they smile it makes you grin
You can't help but give a second look
At those chocolate candy eyes
At lips that surprise
With hair so soft it floats on air
You try your best not to stare
But what can you do
When love stands in front of you
Barefoot in blue jean skin
My heart must give in
To this oasis of beauty
That makes my head swim
Now when I dream I

Dream for two
Everything is what I want for you
Forever, For ever
Always together
For love is not the question
Love is the answer

Note: I wrote a poem using Blue eyes as a standard of beauty and you said, 'why is it always blue eyes', so, I've written poems of grey, green, and brown as well.

Emerald Green

Written: April 13, 2014

I feel like I'm in
The presence of a siren queen
A beauty with eyes of emerald green
They draw me closer
Dazed as like a dream
I can't turn away
Trapped by the emerald green
Of a siren queen
I know I need escape
But I no longer control my fate
As those green eyes draw me to her shore
And though my heart may strike her rocks
I care no more

Shadowy Eyes

Written: April 13, 2014

You see her from a distance
A beauty that breaks down all resistance
Then up close she brings a surprise
With those eyes
Eyes that are grey as slate
Those eyes stop you
And hold you, drawing you onto her shore
Make you wait till you're sure
It's safe to ask for that first date
And you know it's something special
When she lets you bring her home late
Those eyes they won't let you go
You see them when you fall asleep
And again at daybreak
You search for them on every face
But there is no one that can replace
Those shadowy eyes
As grey as slate

CHARLES WAYNE CUMBIE

Honey Bee No Memory

Written: April 28, 2014

It's a fine day
A southern comfort temperature
Warm gentle breeze
Rustling in the trees
A happy sight
Honeysuckle bushes
Covered in honeybees
It brings a smile to see their flight
Survivors of the blight
The worker bee hard at it
Kindred spirits are we
Working hard just to be
A little free
The honeybee takes from the flower
So the hive may thrive
But a thankful harvester is he
For in trade with pollen
He gives them life
So, the bee and the flower
Share their lives together
Like lovers entwined in a dance
A southern comfort romance

I Met a Girl and it Made All the Difference

Written: June 15, 2014
Dedication: To my wife Debbie, on our 40th anniversary

40 years ago I met a girl in Oregon
In the small town of Tillamook
It was there she took and kept my heart
The sun did shine on her flowered hair
And I knew I loved her then and there
We both fell in love under that big ocean sky
So, together we joined our lives forever
Saying I do and yes to whomever
We shared the sunny days
Enjoying our love no matter the weather
So, now we set in the twilight of our love
I have such fond memories of
My life with you my love
I number my days and wish there were more
To spend with you, the one I adore
I'm so glad we met
We have spent four decades
Of sharing and caring
And raising our family together
We broke the pattern and saved
The best wine for last
Soon, now our time will be ours again

CHARLES WAYNE CUMBIE

Not having to share with the man
Might there be a second honeymoon in the plan
Come with me and take my hand
We will fan the flame of our love
Until the memories are bright again

My wife and I

If Beauty had a Name

Written: June 28, 2014

Today I met a butterfly who wasn't shy
In the summer sunlight
The butterfly danced on the air, so light
It was a fairy's flight
Floating softly out of sight
But to my surprise and my delight
She circled back up close to me
Dancing on the air
Showing off her fairy wings, she was so fair
She must be a she for beautiful was her wing
Yellow gold with black lace
Such a small delicate thing
I've seen her before
She's my neighbor from the tree next door
We both share a love
For the beauty of the land
I wonder if she could feel
That I was her friend
And that is why she floated so near again
A beautiful thing
With her golden black lace wing
I don't know her well enough
To give her a name

CHARLES WAYNE CUMBIE

But if beauty had a name
It would be her
Of the golden black laced wing
Floating and dancing for me
On the warm summer air
Such a beautiful, beautiful, delicate thing
Floating on air with her fairy wings

Dear One

Written: July, 2014

You are the dear one
You introduced to me my children
Helped me name them one by one
You brought into my life a kindness
That has only grown
How could I ever leave you alone
And though I work in the heat and the dust
Far away from any throne
You are my dear one
Who has given me a home
I regret that I have so little to give
But what I have is yours
A caring, a sharing, a giving
A love that will stand up to the test
You, my dear one, bring out my best
And I will never leave you
Even though all my days are gone
And I'm laid to my rest
Still, I will reach for you
With a hand, and a word
And pull you through to my chest
And embrace you
For you are my dear one
And I could never leave you alone

CHARLES WAYNE CUMBIE

New Born

Written: July, 2014

Two lovers danced
Both taking a chance
That in the fertile soil
Of their romance
Soon love would bloom
A legacy born
A future sworn
As the light comes
Into the newborn's eye
And the mother's joy
Is the father's happiness
As he holds with gentle tenderness
This tiny new life
A gift from his wife
And as he gives thanks
He softly kisses the child's cheek
As the tears of joy begin to swell
Such a wonderful gift, this little life
And of their happiness
To everyone they would tell

When You are Close to Me

Written: October 20, 2014

When the day has just been too long
And everything has gone wrong
You look at me with concern in your eyes
That's when I know you love me
You are my anchor in the wind
With you I feel like I've had a win
And nothing can bother me again
When you are close to me
Because you are my anchor in the wind
You make me feel like I can try again
Cause nothing can get under my skin
When you are close to me
When I call your name
And hear your sweet reply
I can feel my soul sigh
That is why I know I love you

CHARLES WAYNE CUMBIE

Love

Written: November 25, 2014

When the angels sing from above
It's your name I will hear my love
When the dawn breaks and the storm calms
You'll be found in my arms
All things are lost in the past
Nothing can last
But the circle of my love
Surrounds you and will hold you fast
For in my world there is no other
Mother, wife, lover
And when you find me standing
In the rain
Waiting for the sun
It's into my arms I beckon you to run
So as the journey must start
I know it must also end
And when we've drank the last drop
May I find you in my arms again

Pursuit of Dreams

Written: December 31, 2014

Life's pursuit of dreams
Now, so far away they seem
If I could I would take you back to the time
When your beauty was free to behold
And our future was still untold
Our memories together, still lingering
Fondly remembering
Though time may dull the ring that binds
And the sands try to dull its shine
Life's pursuit of dreams
Brought you to be mine
And even though far away they seem
Age cannot dull the shine
Together we are like that fine wine
That only gets better with time

p.s. This year's last chance for poetry
2014 is on the way, may next year bring
Enough beauty to behold
That it's easy to ignore the old

Charles Wayne Cumbie

Beauty

Written: January 26, 2015

Beautiful, golden skinned ladies
With the sky in their eyes
They capture you with their
Bright light smiles
I can't tell you wrong from right
Cause the rules they always change
But beauty (its own law remains)
And though time stays the same
Beauty is the celestial drug
That goes down deep within
Not just a superficial skin
It's the bridge where love crosses over
And worlds begin to spin
So, let my opened eye
Drink in the sight
As love crosses over
And two worlds unite

Still Mine

Written: February 10, 2015
Dedication: To Debbie

Forty-one valentines
And you are still mine
Years together our souls entwined
I know your thoughts and you know mine
Our memories so sweet, as mellowed wine
We walk together your hand in mine
On that day we will find
A lover's special place to dine
And speak our thoughts you and me
Of so many years how could it be
Still together we stand embraced
And I see once more the sunset's glow on your face
A kiss in time, and I know you're still mine
And you will always be
My happy valentine

CHARLES WAYNE CUMBIE

Fate Turns

Written: March 29, 2015

Oh! That wonderful day
The day I missed my ride
But I found my bride
Fate stepped in
And now I have
A lifelong friend
I reach for you and
You are there
The world is ours to share
As the clock ticks slowly by
Our memories collect
Up to the sky
You are the one
That makes me sigh
Content to lie
Here by your side
Who could have known
Such a simple thing
A missed ride
And I found my bride
To wear my ring

p.s. fate turns on the smallest of things

Love Sick

Written: April 22, 2015

Hey! Cupid
Stay away from my heart
She's so beautiful
She's a work of art
But I can't fall, I can't fall
It will be too far
She stands in the morning sun
Like an angel with a message to be sung
I hold out my hand, as if to touch
But I know I can't, she's not for real
I wish I could express to her how I feel
But there are no Earthly words
The words I need are surreal
I look and can't help but see
That my heart will never again be free
What you do to me, takes my breath away
I stare in awe at the gold in your hair
And the sky in your eyes
You leave my heart full of song
Oh, well it's too late
Cupid has come and gone

CHARLES WAYNE CUMBIE

Dear Valentine

Written: February, 2016
Dedication: A valentine for my wife, Debbie

Hello, my valentine
Thanks for being so kind
You care for me as I care for you
It's just what valentines do
You smile at me and the shine
In your eyes makes me realize
That our love is as sure
As the sun's rise
The chocolate heart I gift
Is a treat so sweet
But what I truly give to you
My dear dear valentine
Is my heart and soul to keep

Love's Token

Written: March 4, 2016

I love you, I will always love you
The waves of fates open shore
Threw us together
Soul mates for evermore
And as I reach for your hand
And you place it in mine
The softness of your touch so dear
Two lovers, mates to the end
Dream together life's plan
You are my days
The sun climbing thru the bluest sky
You are my nights
The moon's glow haloed by stars' light
Together we summon the children of God
And teach them to hold onto the iron rod
Till the truth reveals, love as the token
That lets the final seal open
And it's over, that wait, so long
As the skies shake with angel song

Sweet, Sweet Jane

Written: May 30, 2016
About: The title is a lyric from a song by Cowboy Junkies

CHARLES WAYNE CUMBIE

Come, walk with me sweet, sweet Jane
We'll find a path that's free
Paved with the soft pink petals of spring
And enjoy the birds on wing
As from the branches they sing
Happy love songs to each other
Nesting together in the sunny spring weather
I'm going to take my time
Enjoy the day with my love, my one and only
When she found me I was so lonely
Oh! My sweet, sweet Jane
I'll take in every moment
While patiently waiting for my appointment
With my sweet, sweet Jane
The tears I have they never came
I did not need to hide them in the rain
She washed away all my lonely pain
With tender kisses that fell soft
Like the summer rain
Oh! My sweet, sweet Jane
Feel my arms hold you
Surround you with my love
Oh! My sweet, sweet Jane
You are my only, my heart's flame
And with you, I need not stand in the rain

Into the Sun

Written: June 15, 2016
About: For our 42nd anniversary

42 years, I go where you go
    And you go where I go
42 years, I give to you
    And you give back to me
42 years, when you fall I help you up
    And when I fall you help me up
42 years, we walk together
    We stand together
    A path of memories soft and deep
42 years, I've watched you sleep
    And together we've had the dawn to greet
42 years, we've watched our children grow
    Watched them play and have some fun
42 years and we're still not done
    A cocoon of love we have spun
    As hand in hand we walk into the sun

CHARLES WAYNE CUMBIE

Beautiful Memories

Written: July 27, 2016

At my life's end
With only memories of where I've been
My fondest thoughts will be of you
Standing in golden sunlight
The ocean breeze blowing your flowered hair
When the days grow too long
And I'm tired and sad with care
Thoughts of you standing there
Cheer me, and lift me out of my despair
How could I have been worthy
Of such a beautiful memory
You standing there, God's work of art
As I from this life depart
It will be this beauteous memory
That will be my last thought
You standing there
Sand at your feet, sun's glow and
Ocean breeze in your hair
How could I have been so lucky, so worthy
To have seen you standing there
God's work of art made with such tender care
You against a canvas of golden light
Standing with a flower in your hair

Grace

Written: November 16, 2016

The summer sun golden on her face
Relaxed and forgiving apart from the race
She moves and I'm captured
Can't turn away my gaze
Nothing I can do to stop the rapture
Fate has set the hardest stone in place
I give freely my all to her
Thankfully, bewildered by her grace
Time begrudgingly lets go and stops in place
As I hold her near and dear
Unwilling to let the feeling fade
A match in heaven has been made
A union of comfort and kindness
A love's union, one of cupid's finest
The love story starts, and heaven takes notice
As together eternity's road is taken
And the tree of life embraces them with its branches
Coupled as one they give life to life
A celestial husband and wife (a timeless love)
Sharing together the wondrous sight
Of that glorious celestial light

CHARLES WAYNE CUMBIE

43 Years Young

Written: June 15, 2017
Dedication: For Debbie on our 43rd anniversary

Debbie,
You came into my life
The mother of my children
The love of my life
My wonderful, wonderful wife
There can be no one above you
For I will always love you
And though the evenings long shadows
Stretch out before us
I will always see you on that beach
With sun and wind and flowers in your hair
And happy am I
With the life with you we've shared
If there comes a time
When a choice is to be made
A choice granted in heaven
I chose you, Debbie
My wonderful, wonderful wife

Goodbye My Love

Written: August 1, 2017

How can I say goodbye
And not make you cry
I know in this life it's late
And I face that final date
For you I would move worlds
And dry every tear
It's just through the years
You have been so very dear
Maybe if I offer kind thoughts
I can ease your pain
You have been a beautiful flower
In my garden of life
Thanks for being there and
Willingly to share
Remember the sunny days
And the beach waves
Remember the good things
The Christmas' and camp outs
The children's laughter
The padding of their quick little feet
Their funny questions of why is the sky blue
You are the sunshine that makes the day
That gives the sky its blue

You are my light, my comfort, my love, my wife
May your tears not be sad tears but loving tears
For you are the most beautiful flower
In my garden of life

Small Valentine Poem

Written: February 14, 2018
About: Small valentine written for Debbie on the wrapping paper from the utensils, we were having a valentine lunch at Elmer's restaurant

When the day is long
And cold shadows seek you out
That's when you long
For the warm sunshine
Of your valentine

44 Years

Written: May 19, 2018

44 years, so long ago
But still remembered though
We long for the fallen years
In memory we honor them with gentle tears
To be young and stay that way
Will have to wait for that promised day
44 years hand in hand
Trying for success at following God's plan
It's a different road to follow
I can see why the iron rod must not be hollow
But together we will weather
All the trouble that blocks our way
There's the grandchildren countdown
A tally that predicts the shortness of our stay
44 years a landmark number
A hill you can plant your flag on
Through the years we have covered a lot of ground
But no matter how far you go
You only get one go round
Still, we'll cling together giving support
As we share our golden years
No matter how short

CHARLES WAYNE CUMBIE

Lonely Soul (Can you hear the Echo?)

Written: September 17, 2018

I could have loved, loved another
But it was you, you and no other
I could have left, left you behind
But I needed to find, find a way
To make a friend, a friend to stay
How could I leave, leave what I had found
Such a treasure, a treasure of the soul
So, I asked you to come, come with me
Always together, together to the end
And as the sunsets, sets on our lives
I will say I could have loved, loved another
But it was you, you and no other
There is such a sadness, sadness in the depths
Of the lonely, lonely soul
Together we fight, fight back the sadness
And are lonely no more, no more
So, we kiss and say goodnight, goodnight
To that darkness of the lonely soul

OTHER

The Family Pet

Written: March 15, 1971
Dedication: For Chubby, my childhood pet
About: This was a short story for my writing class, but felt it belonged.

    We named him Chubby because he was a little on the heavy side. He was the family's first pet, and as it turned out he was our last. There was just no replacing him. I found this out much too late. It's strange how a pet can so easily be taken for granted, and it's only when he's gone that the mistake is realized. Chubby stayed by me from the time I was six till I was twelve, when time--the one enemy no one defeats--destroyed him. I buried him in some nearby woods, and a few years later the city erected a shopping center for his tombstone. To me, he was the proof that dog is man's best friend.

    Chubby was like a thickly built bulldog, but he had the long nose and floppy ears of a hound and was about the same size. He had short light brown hair. His four-inch stub of a tail might have been from the bulldog in him or the result of an accident. Perhaps his previous owner had it cut off. But all in all, he was a decent looking dog and a perfect companion for me. He became my nose, my eyes, and my ears. And when I was afraid, he was my courage.

CHARLES WAYNE CUMBIE

He was truly an American dog, with not a drop of pure blood in him, just one big mixture. And he was also smart. One day when we were out playing in a field, Chubby--having a super talent for discovery--was ploughing through the weeds just ahead of me when he let out a yelp and took off running. He had stirred up a hornets' nest, and we were stung all over. We ran until we were safely away, and finally stopped on a grassy bank. I was stinging all over. Then Chubby did something strange: he started rolling down the bank. I figured he must be doing it because of the bee stings. I said to myself, "Maybe it will help me." So, I tried it. And I'll be dogged if it didn't stop the stinging. And all he ever got from us in return was the table scraps, a long chain around the neck, and an occasional pat on the head.

It's too bad that this great dog went unappreciated. I've regretted it ever since, and I've always wondered how we could have been so blind. His special character could not have been overlooked if we had just taken the time to look. He had an all or nothing approach to life. If I showed him any kind of friendship like a pat, a gift, or just a plain play; he would jump all over me, licking my face, wagging what tail he had, and always barking his appreciation. But if he was extremely friendly to a pat, he was furious to a challenge. I never saw him run from a challenge. Once, when he had followed me to school, he was challenged by three other dogs. Two of them were his size, but the third one was huge, nearly twice his size. He took all three of them on. He went after the big one first and managed to get him by the throat. When Chubby finally let go, the big dog had had enough, and ran for it. Seeing this, the two smaller dogs also turned tail and ran. It was a proud moment for Chubby and a lesson in courage for me. I believe that if he'd been given the chance, Chubby would have fought to his death just to please me and win my affection.

    Chubby was always wanting to please me. I could be playing with him in the backyard, and say, "sick'em boy," or "go get'em," and he would run at top speed in the direction I pointed for about fifty feet; then he would stop and look around for the enemy that my command had convinced him was there. So strong was his faith in me that he would do this over and over again. Always convinced that an enemy was near.

    There is no doubt in my mind that Chubby was special. I was always too busy with my own selfish pursuits. I never did take the time to notice him. But he's gone now, and only in my memories does he still live. I learned much from him, but just as his death taught me to give a friend the appreciation he deserves before it's too late, I know in the back of my head that being in the human race, in the rush of the day, I will most likely forget.

CHARLES WAYNE CUMBIE

My dog Chubby and I

Nothing

Nothing I see as the dark over takes me
Nothing I feel as I await the sedate and lose my grip on the real
Nothing I fear as God approaches near
Nothing is the space between, the glue that holds the seam
Nothing left to live but the last breath I give
Nothing to dream as awake I still seem
Nothing that marks the spot of all that counts a lot
Nothing to lose is so much more to choose
Nothing it would seem fills the cup with a stardust dream
Nothing a tale of woes or the all-important ohs
Nothing is the space that holds the place where balance is found

What Color Do I Paint My Jet?

My day always starts so hard
It's such a chore to get to the edge
Of my big round bed
And touch my feet to the floor

This mirror today showed
Too many hairs out of place
Oh what a chore
It's hard to get the world renowned
Stylist to show before I become an eyesore

CHARLES WAYNE CUMBIE

Shopping's such a chore
I send my servant out the door
And off to the store
Who needs to know what a bar codes for
Not me but my spending is such a chore

Trying to knock that balance down
Every day it seems
Money begets money
My bank account is bursting at the seams

Just the other day a pesky reporter
Asks me what's a barcode
I can't go through life not being able
To answer simple questions like that
I have to get my butler to explain
But I'll have to get my interpreter
Oh, what a chore

What color to paint my jet, oh what a chore
If I paint it blue
They won't see me, and I must be seen
If I paint it black
They'll say I've gone to the dark side
If I paint it green
They might think I'm a brag about my money
See what I mean?

Just Hit'em

Written: August, 2010
About: A golf poem

The goal I seek, a simple cup
The grail of golf, so small
That it must be flagged up
Or fail to find it at all
So, let's tee this ball up
And send it on its way
Fore, I will share its fate
On this great field of play
Such a small toy to bring such joy
One stroke to stand out from all the rest
Giving hope that you're the best
And, as it ends its flight with a bite
And on the green comes to its rest
I'll then do my very best
To putt it home and pass the test
To prove just once that I was best

CHARLES WAYNE CUMBIE

Hurray for the Losers

Written: August, 2010

As the competition draws to its end
And a winner has come in
There can be no more a tie
Hurray for that second guy

For without him there can be
No win, and no champion
So, make sure to not forget
That if there's one that's won the bet
It is the second one in play
That has made possible that victory day

Never Give Up

Written: October 27th, 2010

Two fighters were in a ring. One stood proud over his win and the other lay flat on his back, a loser again. The defeated one, exhausted, eyes closed, senses deadened, could still hear the referee's countdown. He didn't mind losing, but giving up, well that was not to happen. He may not be a champion, but he would never give up. So, with an effort of will, the defeated one rolled to his knees and stood up on shaky legs. His right arm felt heavy, so he let it drop and hang limp. The referee leaned in and asked if he could continue the fight. A wordless nod was given, and the fight began again. As the champion closed in, the defeated one raised his left glove in front of his chin to deflect the knockout blow as best he could while buying time for the strength to come back to his right arm. And the blows, though they stung, were not able to quite get to the job done. The defeated one tried to will the strength back into his arm while warding off the punches, to minimize the harm as a rain of blows brought him to his knees. Another ten count was given, the defeated one gladly accept this gift of time, as he felt more strength flow back into his arm. Finally, the defeated one had bought with bruised body the time he needed. His right arm was alive again. He focused all his remaining strength to that arm for he knew he had only one swing left. So, he dropped his left-hand guard and invited the champion in to make his final smashing knockout blow. But what the champion did not know was that he would be well met by the defeated one's last blow. The crowd was stunned into silence, not believing what just happened: the defeated one, who could hardly stand, had struck a fearsome blow that matched the champion's. Both blows landed together, both fighters were felled to the mat, both lying flat for the count of ten; and, no one left to boast a win

Afterword

Line from Ray LaMontagne:
'You may knock a man down, but it doesn't mean he's beat'

The tough ones will get back on their feet and
Grin at you with bloody teeth.

Song of Life

Written: April, 2011

Let's grow our hair long
And learn to play a song
That does the soul good
And swells the heart
Like the breakfast song
Of the meadow lark
And may our notes of harmony
Float high on the summer breeze
And welcome in the open arms
A love of life that's fully free

CHARLES WAYNE CUMBIE

Taylor Swift

Written: May 26, 2011
Dedication: A tribute to a country singer

Thank you for your songs of love
And for giving the world a much-needed hug
Your songs bring us back to the heart
And keep warm our souls from the cold
Your heart is so full it can't be worn on your sleeve
You must hold it high above for the whole world to see
With such haloed hair and songs of care
You must be from somewhere up there
A God's gift, sent Swift from above
His poetic songstress that with compassion He deemed to share
To comfort a world suffering in despair
You teach those who want to be so mean
To love a little more, for such kindness is hard to ignore
Your songs warm our hearts, and make us glad
Bringing us closer to the day we forget how to be sad
And as your songs of love and kindness turns the world to face a better place
Swift, will be the chant of the crowd as they praise aloud your name
Taylor, their adoration to suit your fame,
And forever on their lips will be your honored name

Such A Little Thing

Written: June 9, 2011

A missed turn, a path not taken
And a soul is lost and turned around
But fate steps in with all its grace
And reveals the place
Where love is found

Love sparked and grown many years tall
Then a little thing so small
It floats on air and rots the roots
And love dies in despair

The little things that glue it all
Birthdays remembered and forgotten
Holidays both big and small
Tell all of love's way
Here to stay or gone away

It's sad that the little things
Matter more than all
They can point and judge
No matter how small

A people created for the law
Punished severely for any flaw

A perversion of that ordained law
Authored by the highest of all

CHARLES WAYNE CUMBIE

Jackie Marie Evancho

Written: June, 2011
Dedication: A tribute to a 10 yr old, littlest opera singer

The heavenly hosts must be smiling
As you sing with voice uplifting

A voice so dear you can feel
The angles draw near
To be close to one of their own

Your angelic voice draws every ear
Near to you
And they all stand up as witness
To the amazing thing you do

Every note to perfection
Perfectly clear
Leaves a longing for more to hear

God embraces this child so dear
And with his grace calms her fear
As she stands on the stage
At such tender age

As her song of love soars high above
And comes to its end
Her beautiful voice has once again
Made the crowd her friend

Comfy Nest

Written: October 1, 2011

The world is lovely down below
But I'm too comfortable to go
Reluctant am I to leave my nest
But the hunger calls to me and insists
That I take to the hunt
I can no longer resist
So, I drop from my nest
Hug the air
Feel it beat against my breast
Tis food I seek that with its
Death brings life
A mouse, a snake, a worm at least
Maybe not a feast
But enough to keep death's door closed
I will spare my dear gentle, tender, reader
The gory details of my airy quest
That allows me to ingest
But I will say it was fussy and
Tickled going down
Now, I must leave the ground
For it's not safe to hang around
So, it's three hops
I pull the air to me again and soar
Up and up back to my comfy nest
To have myself a pleasant snore

High above the forest floor
Secure and safe in my favorite tree

Inventor

Written: 2012

The inventor sets and he visualizes
What has never been
The idea approaches from within
Appears like a skeleton
That he must flesh out
His mind can see it just so
But he does not yet know
How to shape it like dough
For its parts cannot be bought
But must be made from scratch or found
In the world around
As the broken things of the world
Becomes his shopping mall
They are seen in a new light
And become the donors that bring
His idea to life
The various bits and pieces
Of the broken down
Are reshaped to live again
In the new idea he's found

Tee it Up

Written: November 19, 2013

Tee it up
Going for the cup
Split the wind
Make it's flight bend
The flash of blade
Will not see the shade
It's in the sun
That the game is won
From the very start
Play with heart
At the end of day
Be able to say
It was a fair play
It's the only way
To stand in the sun
Where the game is won

CHARLES WAYNE CUMBIE

Small Beach Poem

Written: January 20, 2014

Under the unbent sky, vast, vast to the eye
Ocean and wind moving their way again and again
The wave comes in to carpet the sand
Coming near but not to touch
Like a friend to say hi and bye again
The breeze brings the thoughts of blossoms
And warmth and coolness to the skin
The two like brother and sister laughing
The ocean and the wind

The Master Eraser

Written: March 3, 2014

Once there was a man
A not so important man
But he did have a plan
An important plan
A plan that would make
The world understand
That this not so important man
Would soon be seen to outstand
Amongst his countrymen
He would poke his finger
Into the eye of history
With his white out
He would strike out
The famed ones inserting
His name to claim their fame
So, when he wanted to be the best
Out would come his white out
To eliminate the rest
And when it was time to be a hero
Out would come the white out
And he was no more a zero
He was the Master Eraser
With his white out

CHARLES WAYNE CUMBIE

And the jot of a pen
He controlled his fate
He could always win
Then one day the plan
With its plot began to thicken
He went to the papers and wrote in
His eulogy that announced his end
But out came the white out and his pen
And the Master Eraser
Walked away with a grin

A Dollar for the Plate

Written: March 29, 2014

I saw the preacher begging
For a dollar for his plate
"Come on now, buy a ticket"
To that faraway place
You know you're gonna go there
Nobody wins that race
Come on place a dollar in the plate
Fold it nice and neat
Buy yourself a padded seat
Get down close to that front row
Be the first to know
Who goes up and who goes down
Believe as little or as much as you want
But of this no one can get around
You must and will go up or down
So, place a dollar in the plate
Fold it nice and neat
Get yourself a front row seat
To that gospel show
Maybe you'll be the first to know
If it's up or if it's down
That you will go

CHARLES WAYNE CUMBIE

Thoughts for a Skier

Written: March 29, 2014

May you stay on your skies with
    No rocks
        No trees
            No sudden stops
Stay sane and remember you're not an airplane
When you're facing three feet of fresh
You can't resist
You know you're going to press it
To the limit
As you give it your best
You feel the joy of the fall
And give it your all
You reach for where
The eagles fly
Your cares like you become weightless
As you float the ride
And hold the edge against
A clear blue sky
As you glide through a cloud of white
With speed and lift you take flight
And admire the world below
As it seems to slow
Then gently you return
To the soft white snow

p.s. A poem for Dale Johnson, snowboarder extraordinaire

When the Seagulls Walk

Written: 2014

I saw the seagulls walking, and I know why
The wind was so strong
It could steal the words from a song
You know you don't want to go outside
When the seagulls would rather walk than fly
The seagull lives his life by the sea
Free to take to the air without a care
Some in defiance tried to put up a fight
And take flight
But instead just hovered there
Giving me a sideways stare that said
I guess I'm going nowhere
So, what a strange sight to see
The seagulls walking right beside me
Even on the ground the wind pushed them around
Teaching them a new kind of walk
I'm sure they would have given the wind
A piece of their mind, if only they could talk
I couldn't help but give a chuckle
Seeing them do that sideways shuffle
Looking so disgusted while the wind happily gusted
I could only stare and smile at their plight
A noble seabird, the wind who was their friend

CHARLES WAYNE CUMBIE

Had stolen their flight
So, I thought, "well fellas it's going to be a
Long walk home, you better get an early start"
But, the noble bird showed me he was too smart
For that, he would just wait it out, so he sat
To the noble bird, who was so grounded
I would have, in respect, taken off my hat
But the wind had blown it away
So that was that

p.s. If you think this poem is interesting enough to share then please do; but, if not, well... then just keep it under your hat.

A Beautiful Day

Written: June 2014

It's a beautiful day
The kind of day that
Tastes sweet like
Ice cream crunch
The kind of day
That makes you want to
Pack a picnic lunch
A day where all the minutes
Are yours to own
No company car
Or business loan
No doctors' way
Just an apple a day
A day that makes
You feel at home
No more being alone
A day where sadness
With a song
can be chased away
If only for a moment
But a moment's all we have anyway
So, listen to your favorite song
Maybe even sing along

CHARLES WAYNE CUMBIE

When the music sinks into you deep
You will feel much lighter
On your feet
Then God's gift of the day
Will be yours to keep

In 1989 Country Went Pop

About: Taylor Swift story
Written: June 6, 2015

The day country went pop
Left some folks in shock
But then the songs that rained down
Were so good, like mana for the soul
She sang and danced till there
Was no frown to be found
Oh, country would miss her
They said as much
But, now she was all grown
And ready to be on her own
So they let her go with a
Comeback again some time
All were happy for her
And wanted to see her shine
That was her "1989"
When country went pop
And no one felt it a crime
The music was good
That's all that mattered
Songs from the heart sung the
Way they should
Words ringing true steeped in the rhythm
When country went pop
All loved the music and all was forgiven

CHARLES WAYNE CUMBIE

Now I Know the Art of Memory

Written: September 4, 2015

When the numbers have faces
You can remember their places
The mind loves a show
Anything you want it can stow
But the memory is the happiest
When the show is the messiest
Noisy and funny the crazier the scene
Makes the memory that much more keen
So, create and enjoy your show
Even chuckle and laugh as you go
Then you will be rewarded
With all that you know

Sweet Madness

Written: November, 2015

Ah, Don Quixote, his was a noble sweet madness where honor and chivalry were held high for all the Gods to see. His personal windmills, a test of his mettle, where his fears were held at bay by the shield of his bravery is a madness that every soldier in every war takes with him into battle. The need to rise up against all who oppose until, in the throes of such madness, no one can stand on the blood-soaked slippery mud. But Don Quixote's madness was of a noble quest to prove honor and chivalry were the best. Riding on the shoulders of the brave he stood above all the rest. Fighting for the weak and the oppressed is the kind of noble madness that the world needs more of. To all the Don Quixote's of the noble quest I say, "May you find favor with the Gods and be blessed." When you dream, might you as well dream big and drink deeply from life's wishing well, striving to put meaning to life with a passion that dusts off the human spirit giving strength to bring life's defeat to its knees. May your chivalry and honor be rewarded with heaven's Olympic gold and may your legends in song be told. Oh you, the good knights, who take up the quest of the noble sweet madness.

p.s. Don Quixote was the first film Debbie and I watched together

CHARLES WAYNE CUMBIE

Fast Food

Written: March 13, 2016

Fast food, what's it good for?
Makes you fatter than before
Fast food is so tasty
It will make you too hasty
And down the calories will go uncounted
Till the worrisome scale is mounted
And then too late you see your mistake
Oh, well die, die, dead, dead
There's a sweet tooth in my head
And as I spend my dough on that expresso
I lay claim to my new name
Dough boy was here not kilroy
The fast food may be fast
But it will slow you down
Till you're the one who shows up last
And in the mirror frown
In desperation you might try to fast
But you know your will cannot last
You can exercise the soles right off your feet
But all that effort is swept aside
When you biggie size
And at the mirror you groan
At the sorry sight of a belly grown
And must admit that you are the one
That's biggie sized

p.s. I would have liked to find some rice paper to write this on. It would have made a nice snack when I was done.

Computer Vs Books

Written: December 22, 2015

The computer is here
Our new revelator and seer
Ones and Os
No more counting on toes

But then again, a better sage
Might be in the page
With its feel of real
The touch of its cover

The box sits and waits
While you try and guess
What you want or need
But where's the fun in that
When carpeted aisles await you to explore

The smell, the touch, of the books of lore
The knowledge goes on wall to wall to ever
Unexpected discoveries made
As you feel their covers
And read the names be it hard back or paper or fancy leather

CHARLES WAYNE CUMBIE

When the storm takes away the light
And leaves your box with a cold stare
You can still cuddle in your chair
Warm by the fireside with book by candlelight
And listen to the words of your favorite
Authors there, the book can take you anywhere

But even though the computer is an awesome foe
The book can hold its own against storm and snow
When the computer fails
The book still prevails

The printed word on scented page
A noble sage for any age

Knight's Eye

Written: March 26, 2016

I am the watchful knight
Never sleeping
Always watching into the night
For that droopy eye
That brings on that restful sigh

I am the watchful knight
With my warding sword
I bare my arm and summon
Only the safest, happiest dreams
Through my bedroom door

I am the watchful Knight
Always making sure
That my golden dream's slumber
Is not disturbed by rude snore

I am the watchful knight
Sentinel who marches
At the heart beats count
Feeling the pressure of day breaks chore
Keeping record of life's deadly score

CHARLES WAYNE CUMBIE

I am the watchful knight
Listening for the sound of any creaking door
Or lightly tread steps
Whose alarm I can't ignore
I am the watchful knight
Never sure of the new day's light
Will it come or will I go peacefully
Into the night

I am the watchful knight
Oh! Happy sound that rude snore
Insuring hence that waking yawn
Will greet the golden rays of dawn

p.s. Near the end of the poem it starts to get dark, but in the end, I let some light in.

The Black Box

Written: June 22, 2016

The black box is recording it all
Right down to the end of my fall
I have my helmet and mike on
And out the planes door I have gone
There is no chute in my pack
Just the black box on my back
Life's lost all its fun
Such a chore it has become
Just tired to the bone, all energy gone
That's why I went out that door
The terror of what's coming at me
I push aside as I take my last ride
On the wind to ground from the sky
The world with its morbid thirst
Will want to know my last thoughts, the worst
So, I think of nothing but feeding the black box
So, here I come no time for the light
For at the end of this flight
I'll be crashing thru death's door
And, when I hit earth's floor
Will it jar open heaven's door?
In the dust of my wake
Will I have long to wait?

CHARLES WAYNE CUMBIE

Or will my messy death leave me stuck
A ghost caught in between
By only the believer's eye to be seen
In the narrow focus of my imminent death
Unnoticed was another at the door when I left
What?!
Caught from behind by my parachutist friend
I should never have talked about my planned end
Oh well, that's how it goes with mice and men
My black box end, spoiled by a friend

p.s. Some say talking about it, is a cry for help
Perhaps my subconscious mind was a sly as a fox
But you have to admit, I did commit, to that black box

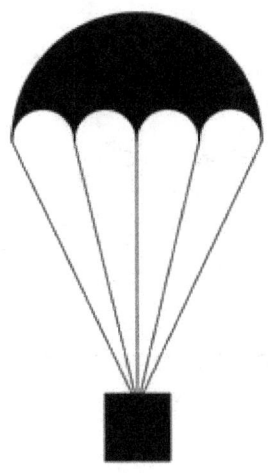

Plan B

Written: August 21, 2016

Was it a suicidal plan B
That inspired the man
Of the fatalistic time
Who wrote the famous rhyme
To be or not to be

Or the exit plan B
To Canada we flee
From that rich man's mercenary war
Eventually a nation's guilty conscience
Brought forgiveness and their sons
Were restored

If there is no plan B
Then the nukes will fly
And it's off to the caves we hide

Everyone needs a plan B
If things go badly wrong
You need to see a way to step aside
Away to flee

CHARLES WAYNE CUMBIE

And, if your life's dream
Vanishes into thin air like steam
A plan B will help you turn the corner
To a new way and another day

The only one that I might see
That doesn't need a plan B
Is the worker bee you see
For he already has a plan, Bee
And he keeps it in his hive
In a cone in his home
Insurance to stay alive

So, even the almighty needed a plan B
When he gave that fateful decree
And said, "Flood them all till they're dead."

So, don't step out your door
Without your plan B
The hidden key that will insure
That you're not left standing
Outside your door

Seasoning

Written: October 4, 2016

There's a time for every seasoning
But there's only so long you can diet
Before you must give in
To that time for every seasoning
When the taste buds and sweet tooth get together
And gang up on you
That's when you have to find
Something tasty to chew
It's a time for ever seasoning
No use feeling guilty
Can't help it, that Hershey's bar is so chocolaty
And the drying sugar plums are not in your head
But are so sweet in the mouth
And on the tongue
There goes the blood pressure
There goes the cavities
There goes the heart as the waist swells
Your lack of control is such a disgrace
But if you die you know
It will be with a smile on your face
So, with open mouth I embrace
A time for every seasoning

CHARLES WAYNE CUMBIE

Inspiring Tale of Grace

Written: June, 2017
About: Inspired by Grace VanderWaal

This is the story about a little twelve-year-old girl of biblical tones
From the mouth of babes' wisdom will come
She sings of friendship, a beautiful thing
Having hope enough to light your sky
And those who refuse to see hope can close their eyes
Be true to yourself, finding yourself, and knowing your name
Not letting others put you down or make you feel ashamed
Not letting half-truths and lies cloud your skies
Not letting others change you into something you are not
Making sure the who of you is never forgot
When she sings, her magical voice
Sinks the message deep into the soul
You can't help but sing along
When she gives you that healing song
A voice that reaches deep within
Makes you feel happy again
A sad ache and a happy shake
Though she may be young in years
She can still bring on the healing tears

Boondocking (A Poem of Freedom)

Written: April 1, 2019

I boondock my earth ship
Giving the Man the slip
Out of sight, out of mind
All I have is time
And it's all mine

It's off the grid I go
All the useless stuff I throw
Having gotten rid
Of the clutter in my life
My Earth ship and I are light
And we take flight

Out into a world that's free
My life is now in the wind
It's freedom that I win
A return to the lazy days of youth
No longer slaving for a fixed roof

So, off I go to see life's show
It's beautiful out here. I've boondocked
My Earth ship by a lake that is as
Blue as the sky

CHARLES WAYNE CUMBIE

I sit and unwind, plenty of time
To make up my mind, as to what to do
Perhaps sip a hot drink as my eyes
Reflect the golden sunrise
Or scratch man's best friend behind his ears
The list of fun things can be as long as I choose to make it

For I in my Earth ship
Have given the Man his pink slip
His services no longer needed
The alarm clock goes unheeded

So, I and my earth ship are both retired
We set awhile and take a rest by this
Beautiful lake side shore
Until again it's time to go
Down my list once more

p.s. Note to the boondocking reader
though I have never met you
yet I respect you
for taking your brave charge at life
go, go and prove to yourself
the universal truth
THAT MAN IS THAT HE MIGHT HAVE JOY

OLD AGE

One Last Time

One last kiss
One last goodbye
One last time to see you again
One last time is always the end
One livin, one dyin
That's the gift, we've been given
And the wisest to walk among us
Has shown us that it's not the end

Goodbye

I see
The bluest of skies
Green fields
And colorful trees
But it all must go
When I say goodbye
There's no way to stop
It's no good to cry
Even though I'll miss it
There's no getting by
That final goodbye
Though you come to visit
Or come to stay

CHARLES WAYNE CUMBIE

There will be the day
Of that final goodbye
The glass is not half empty
Or half full, it's just empty
When you are one of the ones
That has to say goodbye

Silver Hair

Silver hair, a life of care
No longer standing far from that heavenly stair
Everything you do is sore and slow
The days are fast on the go
Most everybody I know
Have stepped onto that heavenly stair
Someday soon now I will awake
And step onto that heavenly stair
I'll see all my family, friends, and pets there
I was too busy to be aware
Of how sad it came be down here
What a heart break it must have been
To take that ring off again
You can't help but cry on into the night
But not even an ocean of tears
Will ever bring back the light in her eyes

Have to Go

This old house has gone to pasture
I'd better get right with my pastor
Cause I'm soon to meet the master
I'm old now and can't move any faster

I guess I'm one of the ones that has to go
The hour is late
My time is near at hand
The sun use to rise for me
But now it sets, to set me free

The Long Shadow

I saw my shadow in the morning light
Guess that means another cold one tonight
My shadow is longer now than it used to be
Another shot across my bow
Time's warning to me
That the days can be numbered now
But I ignore and go on, pretending anyhow
I do still have a shadow, do I not
Though it be long and threatening
I will cherish my moments in the sun
Me and my shadow on the run

CHARLES WAYNE CUMBIE

Waking Up

I woke up old again today
The long shadows of time
They weigh heavy on my mind
My daily hills get harder and harder to climb

I woke up old again today
But there's a pill for every ill
So I don't feel the chill
Of that reaper's breath sneaking up behind

I woke up old again today
But the wisdom of age came to save me
So I began to look for him
This invisible one has been so close
All around me, all my life
All I had to do was look with unveiled eyes
And there he was in every face

Just close your eyes
And say the prayer *Father are you there?*
And when you look again you will find him
Watch then and look at the people
And you will find the image of him
In every kind word
In every helping hand

Last

Written: Summer, 2010

The old man was lying in his bed for the last time. Barely awake, dreaming his last dreams of younger days when no bed could hold him. The doctors in their white coats were counting down the time for his last breath, for time was money and the beds were expensive. Their thoughtlessness bespoke of how little they were aware that all too soon their time too would come and then his bed they'd share.

Good Bye

Written: September, 2010

May the angels keep on singing
Let me follow their sirens song
Back to my first home
'Cause I know it won't be long
Before all my time is gone
And though I long to stay
I know it just doesn't work that way
No more can I hang around
There's no need to be down
Life's just that way
So, you know I think it's time
That I found some higher ground

So, open up that brightened sky
You won't find me too shy
To say goodbye

Final Goodbye

Written: September, 2010

And, as the golden years turn to tears with the approach of the final goodbye, I reflect and realize they're all gone now with closed eyes: Mother, father, brother, grandma, grandpa, aunts and uncles.

All taken by death's plague.

Now, I know the feel of the holocaust as I stand alone, family gone, only memories to keep them alive. Even that is gone with death's final sigh, and when the memories fade from my dimmed eye, that will be the final goodbye.

POEMED | OLD AGE

Travel Bag of Life

Written: October, 2010

Soon I will have to pack up and go
I had a life though, but now it's gone
I had some fun, that's gone too
All that's left are the memories of you

When I go I can't take gold
When I leave I'll leave alone
But, what I take is what's my own
The memories of you and home
This is what I truly own
The memories of a life that's gone

So, with this little time that's left
Come with me to that ocean's shore
We'll feel once more the cooling breeze
As we watch the waves of that blue green sea
Then hand in hand we'll go explore
And pack up a few memories more

And when I leave because I'm old
They'll be nothing I can hold
But the memories all packed to go
So, together we'll pack the bag full

And for those who will miss me don't cry sad tears
For I have packed my travel bag full through the years
With memories that I truly own
And I'll unpack it again when I get back home

Old, So Old

Written: February, 2011

I look in the glass, can't believe what I see
Looks like not much is left of me
This horse I'm riding is about to throw me to the ground
And there's not much left when I look around
All I can see is a shell of me
So, soon I must go
I would like to take you with me, need the company
But where I go it's just not easy to follow me
It's scary, this dead-end road I'm on
Will I be brave enough when my last moment's gone?

POEMED | OLD AGE

The Box

Written: June, 2011

Some may think this is my last home
The four sides and a lid of a life that's gone

And the last sound this soul will hear
Is the hammering on ….
And a few words of a goodbye song

But as that last shovel full puts a period to my life
And the third sun is gone and hid from sight

I feel my soul drawn forth into the son's light
And the angel's song guides me back
To my true home

So, say your words and sing your farewell song
For a life that's now gone
But it won't be for long

Just listen for the sound of that Gabriel's horn
And you know it will be the sound
Of a new life that's born

CHARLES WAYNE CUMBIE

Sad Eyes

Written: August, 2011

Sad eyes of a life spent and gone
Sad eyes that for youth do long
You turn away and shake your head
But the reflection does not lie
There's nothing more that can be said
Just the sad eyes and a goodbye
What do I do now the best days are gone?
Nothing left but a geriatric swan song
And a yearning for youth
That's long gone

Tired and Retired

Oh no, looks like I forgot to shave my face
Now I'll be a human disgrace
Look, I don't even wear the right clothes, not even underwear
No way for a man to dress
I haven't cut my hair in over a year
I guess people will stare and think
There goes a man in distress
Oh wait, why do I worry
I'm retired

POEMED | OLD AGE

Free and Retired

Written: September 3, 2011
About: A Retirement Poem

When I'm retired, I'll...
Eat when I want
Sleep when I want
Wander around doing fine
Take my own sweet time
No hurry, no rush
Sleep in my clothes if I must
Do my laundry standing in the rain
No one needs to know my name
There's no shame in standing idly by
The rich man takes and does the same on the fly
When there's a cloudless sky
I go outside
No cubby hole to be held by
All the time in the world is mine
Plenty for counting stars or brushing the leaves
A time for admiring the work of the master's hand
I know with him my glass will never run out of sand

CHARLES WAYNE CUMBIE

So It's Your Birthday

Written: October 20, 2011
About: Sort of a parody of John Lennon's 'So this is Christmas'

So it's your birthday
And another year gone bye
We wish you a happy birthday
Without any goodbyes

The cake is all lit for you
'Cause you are the star
May time stand still for you
And leave you unscarred

So it's your birthday
The end of another year
We hope all your loved ones
Have gathered near

As each candle is lit to mark the time
May the brightness of the light
Warm your heart like
The golden sunshine

The Misty Mist

Written: December 24, 2011

Your dearest moments
Are your saddest ones
When all you've done
Has come and gone
The memory of your day
Slipped away
Into the misty mist

No one can know of all the you
That has been
For it's all hidden in
That misty mist

I call the names of those
Long lost to me
I see their faces
In the misty mist of memory

Ones dear and loved
Now too far to touch
Held captive in that misty mist
I alone remain and hold close to my breast
The dear ones that I know best

CHARLES WAYNE CUMBIE

And cart them away
Into that misty mist
It's been said there will be a time
When all will be found, and none lost
But till then I keep them safe here
In that misty mist of memory

POEMED | OLD AGE

Bone Garden

Written: March 5, 2012

I've got to get back to where the seagulls fly
To watch the clouds sail by
Before God's pointing finger says die

I've entered that no go home zone
Where my age has set the exit stage
That once I leave my door behind
I may not be able to once again find
The strength to walk the path that leads back home

I stand in the bone garden with its sprouts of stone
Gaze about to try and find my rest alone
And as I see these Earth forgotten ones
The thought bores down
That these hopeless ones planted here deep in the ground
No sound they make with their endless wake
Have no hope of a morning's rise
Be it only one mentioned by the wise
A risen son who will kiss awake
Those left behind, he did not forsake

CHARLES WAYNE CUMBIE

Vision Eyes

Written: August 9, 2012

Dead, gone
Can't speak with them no more
They keep silence in their sleep
With vision eyes I look back
To when there were bluer skies
With no tears to blur the eyes
Only smiles and sweet memory
There is nothing I can do or say
That will bring back those lost days
I only can look back with
Vision eyes to try and feel
The memory of those smiles
And bluer skies

Bluesy

Written: January 7, 2013
About: My first blues song inspired by watching the Son House Blues Man... Not sure how much of this is my words or the words from someone else's song.

You know
I'm going to that one suit town
Won't need no looking round
Cause I can't be found

You know
You can't get more down
Than the one suit town
It'll make you frown

You know
Your tickets punched
When they set you in the ground
With that one suit on

You know
You won't be taking nothing with you
But that one suit to the
One suit town

CHARLES WAYNE CUMBIE

You know
Looks like I'm one of the ones
That has to go
To that one suit town

The Old Man

Written: March, 2013

The old man stood on top of a treeless hill
Weak and out of breath, the only way he made it was by sheer will
He stood there, catching his breath, looking out over the four horizons
Thankful for the tears that washed away his fears

Cold

Written: October 28, 2013

It's getting cold and it's hard to see
It's time to pay life's fee
I guess this is it, the room appears
So dimly lit
And when the silence comes
Will you remember me?
It wasn't long these numbered days
Now the night has come
And I forgot to enjoy the play
Can there be a happy ending
To an end
Maybe someday they'll pray the
Life back into me and hopefully
I'll walk and talk again
With you on some sunlit day

CHARLES WAYNE CUMBIE

Shady Ghost

Written: November 16, 2013

This horse I'm riding is beginning to stumble
All that sand can sure make a man humble
It'll bring you trouble
Make you lose your home
It'll take you downtown
Leave you in the ground
You'll look around
But I won't be found
Put your ear to the breeze
Who knows, you might hear me sneeze
Then you'll know
It's not just the leaves waving at you
When you hear those footsteps behind you
But there's nothing to see
Then you'll know how much it was that
I didn't want to leave

Free at Last

Written: January 5, 2014
Dedication: To Chad and Ken, young at heart

He woke up with a start
The window showed it was no longer dark
He looked at the clock and knew it was late
He must have forgot to set that alarm
And like Alice's rabbit would have to rush
Or miss his important date
Now, he was in a hurry, everything was a worry
He rushed to get there
Forgot to comb his hair
Nor had time to shave
They would think he knew not how to behave
And then, oh, no, that you're late whistle he heard blow
He sat up still in his bed
A look of relief replaced the dread
And he remembered he doesn't have to
Worry or be in a hurry
Because he's free, you see
He's a retiree
Though he may be on a dead-end road
At least no longer can the workers'
Treadmill make him bow down and bend
Because he's free as free as the wind

CHARLES WAYNE CUMBIE

As I Go By, I Pass Away

Written: January 14, 2014

As I go by, I pass away
The distance grown till I can't say
I'll ever be back to see what
God's time eraser made
A newness already on the fade
I can only say that I have been
With voice now carried away on the wind
As I go by and pass away
I look on the future as bright sunrise
But mostly I fear the aged tired eyes
Will miss what God's time eraser made
Fore time has no short or long
For what's gone is now new
And what's new is now gone

Masterful Illusion

Written: March 23, 2014

O death, that masterful illusion
The master's sleight of hand
That no one can understand
Until it falls upon them
At the gallows edge
The truth revealed by death's dredge
The newly opened eye
Sees the illusion's lie
But you can't go back to speak this truth
For you are cloaked in the vail
So, for the old world
Knowledge must fail
And faith drawn up
From the depths of the soul
Like buckets from the well
Gives water to the seed
That tells the tale
Of illusion broken
By the toll of the death knell

Slow-Mo

Written: May 5, 2014

When I finish this job
I promise I'm gonna slow down
Maybe take slow walks
And for the first time really see this town
Maybe sit on the benches
And watch life's show
Not so fast, now in slow-mo
Get off the treadmill and into
The audience, at last
I've worked so long that
Everything is in the past
Gotta make these last few last
Take the time to enjoy
God's masterful hand
Take in all the scenes of green,
Smell the pinks and whites of spring
Thankful that I can still hear
The children laughing in the park
To see such happiness
It brings on a smile
That lifts the heart

Enjoying God's Retirement Plan

Written: August, 2014

No more wasted days
No sweat off the brow
It's back to the garden
A sun dance craze
A cool moon phase
Humbled am I
At the beauty of the sky
That holds the beautiful butterfly
And all the creatures
That want to fly
I'll watch as God's hand
Reveals his plan
And the rainbowed sky
Gives hope to the land
That the world will still stand
I'm in the midst of all this beauty
No longer a slave to mankind's duty
I taste, I smell, I wait to hear God's bell
Calling me to come drink from his well
But, what can I say
But that this is my day
I'll spend it with all the love
And compassion of a simple free man
Enjoying God's plan revealed by his hand

CHARLES WAYNE CUMBIE

The Countdown

Written: September, 2014

I've entered the 'old zone'
Everything I do starts with a groan
Now every day counts
Count your pills
Count your calories
Count your chills
Count your doctor bills
Count your blessings
Not too many left
Most worn out and gone
So, when you've entered
That old zone
Make sure to take time
To see what's on
For time is short, sorry but
I can't finish this poem
It's time to go take some more pills

So, It's Your Birthday Version 2

Written: September 29, 2014

So, it's your birthday
Another year gone
We wish you a happy birthday
With this birthday song
May your next years be good ones
And prolonged
May all your loved ones
Come to celebrate your day
And may the angel of happiness
Come here to stay

CHARLES WAYNE CUMBIE

Downstream

Written: November 5, 2014

I watch the petals of the dead
Float by, current drawn
My thoughts with them are led
To wonder where they've gone
Do they seek the lair of the dead?
There is only one way to know
I must dawn upon myself death's cloak
And in the dying feel the cold current
Soak and drench the soul
Till it's sodden down and sinks to drown
Following the cold current down
Till the lair is finally found
And there to lie not in despair
But free of all care
Until a shining day dries out the
Sodden soul and makes it shine and smile again
No more need to lay
But to rise up to the surface
Of a new born day

Will It Be

Written: November 19, 2014

What will be left of me
Will it be a memory
Some kindness I gave
Will it be a line of poem
Unshakable from memory
Will it be me in my youth
Or so, very, very old
In a hundred years will
There be anyone to know
What do you do when you've
Outlived your past
And the future's always just
Out of grasp
The present holds you still
And bends down your will
All three ghosts haunt your soul
While you wait for the light
To say it's time to go

CHARLES WAYNE CUMBIE

<u>Retired</u>

Written: December 2, 2014

When I retire it will feel like
The return of Pooh to the 100-acre wood
To see again the lazy summer days of my youth
A time to chase butterflies again
Except this time only with my eyes
A time to seek out the blue of a cloudless sky
And to turn around and watch with a wizened eye
This time with no clock to interrupt the joys of the heart
I will visit and linger all day in the beautiful park
No need to start or end
Just taste and savor the moment you are in
Count those flowers
Say hi, to the children
Bask in the energy of that youth
That beams your way
You can't stay old when everyone's at play

Shake Rattle and Roll

Written: February 10, 2015
About: Inspired by an old couple I saw at lunch one day

I see the elderly couple
Finish their meal and get up to go
But even though the years are heavy
And they move slow
He still holds the door for his one love
The cup of ice he holds
Shakes with a quivering hand
His wife's walker gives a rattle as it rolls
It's a new kind of "shake rattle and roll"
Still together these many years
In good company they stroll
The sound they make is a new kind of
"Shake rattle and roll"
It's the musical dance of the old
With a slow step, "shake rattle and roll"
Their dance together honors the years
It's a honor roll of a lasting love
Still shared together
The endearing last dance of the old
A new kind of slow step
"Shake rattle and roll"

CHARLES WAYNE CUMBIE

Uphill Both Ways

Written: May 17, 2015

So, you're in your 60's now
Forget the over the hill gang
You belong to the uphill
Both ways gang now
It's not an apple a day
It's a doctor a day
You're on the pill
But not in a fun way
And, for you each chill
May summon the death knell
You're tied to the tracks of life
And when you see that light
At the end of the tunnel
Well, that's life coming at you
So, grease up those walker wheels
And get those tennis balls on
But it's not to the court
You be going, yours is a deadly sport
It's uphill both ways now
So, hold on tight
Cause here comes the light

On the Street (Another Box Poem)

Written: November 6, 2016

Looks like my shoes are worn out
And I need some more socks
I'm so tired of living in this box
But freedom doesn't come cheap
Living on the street
I'm caught in a song's lyric
"Freedom's another word for nothing
Left to lose and nothing left to choose"
I need the blessings of the cleric
Just to make it through another day
But Sunday comes only once a week
And my prospects are so bleak
That hunger is my daily shadow
So, I walk the street
Looking for small lost treasures
The dumpster is my super market
I look for anything I can pocket
Park benches my seat
And doorways my keep
People, they don't mean to be mean
As they pretend I'm unseen
It's just that I'm such a bother
So, scared they are of my unknown

CHARLES WAYNE CUMBIE

Not even a Christian will take me home
As I circle the block
My world begins and ends
With this cardboard box

Epitaph

Written: 2015
About: This poem was inspired by my dad, when he bought flowers enough to completely cover my mother's grave

It was the last gift
Far from that first I do
Beautiful flowers covering you
Though the days be sunny
I'm still blue
Left here without you
I felt so loved when I was with you
Remembering the hard times, you carried me thru
When I talk to you now
It's hard to keep the tears from welling up
For there can be no answer
Just a memory of what I know you would say
A gift of your voice
Would be enough to soften the sadness
And wipe away the tracks of my tears

The Four Horsemen

Written: July 19, 2017

The four horsemen
When they come
Where you gonna run?
You know you're due
When they're sent for you
It's just the end of life
Coming at you
Best you can do is delay the day
Maneuver them into
A death valley corner
Make sure they come at you
One at a time
And you have a chance to unhorse them
One by one
Here's where I must diverge from my poetic realm
You see for me the four horsemen of which I speak are
Prostate cancer, bone spur arthritis,
Heart disease and diabetes
All four of these bad guys
Are lurking in my body
Elbowing each other to be
The first to serve my demise
The cancer can with luck

CHARLES WAYNE CUMBIE

Be unhorsed by the surgeon's scalpel
Likewise for the arthritic bone spur
But the diabetes and heart disease
With luck could be unhorsed by my own efforts with
Diet and exercise provided
My desire to stay alive can
Fuel the will power needed for the deed
So, there you have it the
Four horsemen who come for me
From them I hide behind the
Surgeon's scalpel and pray
For the will to overcome my
Human nature

The Complaint

Written: December 16, 2018

Work all day
Work all night
Work is a chore
Sleep is a fight
Nothing's easy anymore
Not even a chance to snore
Tired I be
Can't sleep easily
Have to work to sleep
It's like a job, using tools
To breathe and water bottles
For dried out mouth and
Up and down twice a night
This is my world, my plight
Goodnight!

Cremation Blend

Written: January 19, 2019

At my end just roll me up and smoke me in
Half hash and half my ash
A cremation blend
At my end call your best artist in

CHARLES WAYNE CUMBIE

Mix my ash into the paint
A cremation blend
Have him paint me young again
At my end toss my ash into the wind
Let the seagulls breathe me in
Listen for my whisper on the wind
At my end pollute the well
With my cremations blend in the pail
Drink me in, let me live again
At my end take my ash
Cremation blend, toss it through creations door
And as my dust his feet kicks up
A ghost of me will rise up
And he will say, "So there you are"
And toss my ash back out the door
To land again on Earth's shore
And from God's good Earth I will arise
To open my eyes to one more sunrise

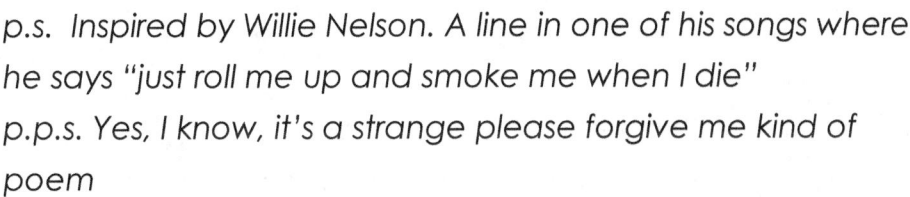

p.s. Inspired by Willie Nelson. A line in one of his songs where he says "just roll me up and smoke me when I die"
p.p.s. Yes, I know, it's a strange please forgive me kind of poem

POETRY

Instructions

How do I write a poem?
You think of something to say
And you say it in a pretty way

What's a Poem?

Written: 2015

A poem is just thoughts put on paper
With a touch of rhyme and a pinch of time
And when the receipt is just right
It will be like opening the shutters
Of a room to the morning light
And you will stretch awake to its warm glow

Why Bother

Written: August, 2010

Why bother with poetry some might say?
Well, a witty line or some flowered words arranged in sweet bouquet
Just might slip out onto the page and sparkle up your day.

Then how eager will you be,
To erase away that boring line,
And brush it clean from memory?
Making way for a worthy rhyme,
That can warm the heart with splendored line,
And liven up your day.

Poetry of a Song

Written: June, 2011

The words of a song might be technically wrong
And look like they might not belong

Some might say that's a mistake
To play on words in that way

But it's not the word or meaning that I take
But the feeling that I make

And that's what gives the head
It's sad or happy shake

A Rhyme in Time (A Poet's Lament)

Written: April 15, 2012
About: This poem is complaining about how I can't rhyme and yet I'm rhyming the whole time

I try and try to write a poem
But, drat it all, I can't rhyme at all
I hear the great one's rhymes
And I'm in awe
'Cause like a stitch in time saves nine
A rhyme in time
Pleases the ear so fine
For a rhyme that creates a cadence I strive
But how to keep a poem alive
If I must make it dance to a tune
But I know if I could, the words would bloom
And their fragrant sound would fill the air
And make one become aware
Of the beauty that is there

CHARLES WAYNE CUMBIE

The One Liner

Written: January 24, 2014

About: Different poem structure, inspired by Chinese writing, giving each word a line unto itself

Oh
Prayer
Oh
word
The
Importance
Of
Can
Only
Be
Known
From
The
Moan
And
Groan
Of
The
Heart
That
Bleeds
Its
Need
To
Atone

Poets' Poem

Written: January 21, 2014

Poe, his cadence will impress
With a style that will make you smile
Rhyming twice a line and once in time
With a rap-tap a heart beat caress

Emily, so majest with words that will
Bend the mind and make it grow
On a word strewn path to her rest

Frost, with words of such beauty
That never in memory can be lost
He'll show you the path to his beautiful wood
And nature's soul will be understood

Whitman, on the epic stage of life he stood
His words like a light held high
To reveal the human sigh
And with an illuminating sweep of understanding
Opens the human eye

Burne, with his field of dreams
Suffered the mouse in his house
Lost but not forgotten to man's schemes

CHARLES WAYNE CUMBIE

His rhymes were the chimes of life
That called to the heart
Like chapel bells
Beckoning the soul to the light

Neruda, sharing love, the beauty of the togetherness, as witnessed by nature's light: sun, moon, sky, my love, my life. "Compartir el amor, la belleza de, la unión, como lo demuestra las naturaleza iluminan, sol, luna, cielo, mia amor, mi vida".

Ehrmann, Desiderata, so long unknown
The gift that hides behind the stone
And in the light is finally shown
The words that speak the essential truths
Offered up free of loan

And, though these poets be long
Dead and gone
With their soulful words
They live on and on

The Poet

Written: December 23, 2013

He can be found in his private lair
Sitting with that distant stare
Waiting for the muse of thought
To give his words a flare
Trying his best to compose with care
Those words that may bare
Some truth to be found there
But he must write, be it good or bad
For it's the diary of his soul to be had
His thoughts, his feelings laid bare
For all the world to like or hate
He stands at their moral gate
And knows he must wait
For their judgement to seal his fate
Will it swing open with wide armed reception
Or clang shut with the shun of rejection
This is the risk he has made
For when the soul cries out onto the page
He must write, be it good or bad
There is no other way or path to be had

CHARLES WAYNE CUMBIE

The Poet Part Two

Written: October 24, 2014
About: On my 64th Birthday

"Dear hearts, and gentle people"
Ah, such a beautiful start
Such a thoughtful beginning
But where is the happy ending
Robbed by the reaper's hand
The poet would not finish his plan
For the beautiful poem
Was left with only a beginning
And now, those who remain among the living
Can only guess at the, might have been,
Left hungry for the soulful meditative end
But with a true beginning
There need be no end
So be it, and amen

p.s. Stephen Foster, 1864, died before finishing his poem at age 37

If there is no Ear to Hear

Written: April 19, 2014

If a poem is never read
It's like it has never lived, it's dead
A soulless mark on the flattest plane
With no spark to start a living flame
I need to say it well
I need to say it right
With the full heart to tell
And words that beckon it to the light
And if, like the Creation, I can shape the words just right
I may even give the dark some light

Poetic Thoughts

Written: December 24, 2014

Whenever I pretend to be a poet, the poems seem to know me and seek me out. As if desperate for a friend, I have to write and let their words on paper shout. But I must wait for my muse: some sight or idea to light the fuse, a special phrase to bring to Earth its weight in the beauty of its worth. So, how can I make the poem stand its test in time if I don't conjure up a worthy rhyme? Sometimes I find that the poem rushes out onto the page, as if it wants to escape its cage. Other times it just seems to say, there's no rush for what it has to say; for if you get the words just right, they can catch the wind and soar high out of sight. So, if you find me stuck here in time struggling for a decent line, to convey what the muse shared today, it's because I must wait to conjure up the magic of the heart to bring light to the dark. Only then, with pen writing furiously fast, might I capture the thought before it takes flight.

Death of a Poem

Written: 11:30 p.m. on January 1, 2015

What voice can raise this poem from the page
Save it from death without age
A poem's story untold, unsung
Condemned to its grave
No loving voice in prayer to save
Love untold and love unsung
Lost, trapped in the page
Like an unsung hero
Unknown, unmarked to his rest laid
For its loss, only tears of sadness
Gone, the heart felt word
Lifting us to our finest hour
Gone the haunting message of the sage
Like the tree in the forest
No sound was made

p.s. First poem of the year 2015. The countdown of my life begins.

Beautiful Words

Written: February 23, 2015

Beautiful words I seek to make the lifeless page speak, to paint mind pictures with words
Beautiful words that can bring joy or sadness and all the memories that give meaning to the past
Beautiful words that hold and keep the memories so they last
Words that put back the sand in life's hourglass
    Oh! How fresh the smell, the sight, the sound
Beautiful words like soft snow that gently settles to the ground
Each flake lit bright like a star light show in the quiet of the night
Beautiful words that keep the memories safe and sound undimmed by time
Beautiful words on a page enshrined can hold the memories of any age
Enduring memories like wine made sweeter with the passage of time

CHARLES WAYNE CUMBIE

Write On

Written: September 23, 2015

As I stand in the shadow of the great ones
With no chance that my words could ever reach their stars
Still I write on, driven by a need to have a say
But even though my words be silenced by criticisms storm
Still I write on till I reach the eye and shake off the cold stare
My words give texture to my untouchable thoughts
And with them I try to harvest the meaning of my life
Must I choose to dwell in hope or in ignored despair
The truth can be found only in the one, not both
The many misty words make it hard to see which it will be
The hope of eternity or the despair of nothing there
It's easier to choose when you have nothing to lose
So, I pick hope with everything to gain
And let despair sink to the depths taking with it, it's sadness and pain

POLITICS

The Plight of the Butterflies

Written: August, 2010
About: An anti-war poem

I know you want to have your war
To take out the best and leave a mess
But if you could delay the fight
Then perhaps you just might
Find the time to be a little kind

So, please don't set the butterflies on fire
For of their beauty one can't tire
As they flit through the air
Without a need or a care

So, please don't set the butterflies on fire
But, if you would or if you might
Take the time to watch their flight
And with a softened heart, belay the fight
And be pleased to not set the butterflies on fire

CHARLES WAYNE CUMBIE

Weep for the Future

Written: September, 2010

Mother Earth, I hear you sighing
For your children are crying
And your Earth is drenched
with the blood of the dying

There is no mass construction for the living
Only mass destruction for the dying
And, you give your plenty freely
Only to be unshared by the greedy

And there's no love for the living
Only hate for the dying
So must, Mother Earth keep on sighing
For her children are crying

Capitalism at Its Best

Written: November, 2010

Born in a country of dreams
Sadly, now, it's a country of schemes
And the man with the gold says
"Do what you're told"
I guess you'd better listen
He'll tell you all the while
With a big sympathetic smile
It's not personnel, just business
And as all the market can bare
Leaves your cupboard bare
And you're left feeling all out of sorts
With his outsource, just remember
It's not personnel, just business
So, when he comes for your first born
And your heart is torn
You can take comfort in the thought
It's not personnel, just business
So, for the man with the gold
I leave for you this thought to dwell
Greed is not leaven
It will lock the door to heaven
And leave you standing in your own hell

CHARLES WAYNE CUMBIE

Capitalism Afterward:
I feel I must share with you this afterthought as well...

I may have been a little too kind
With this capitalistic mind
When I failed to speak about that time
When the guillotine blade did shine
And lopped off the heads that did wine and dine
Sending their moral message to the basket below
"It's not business, it's personal"

Needy Poor

Written: April 11, 2012

Oh, the needy, needy poor
Forced to walk on Earthen floor
No balm for any sore
Wolves circling at their door
What champion will fend for them?
What champion can be found
To hear the anguished cries they sound?
One who bares his arm with gleaming sword
Stronger than any ward
As evil that men do rears up
It surely will lose its head as the sword
Flashes and stings
Till evil is either bled or fled
On its darkened wings
Who steps onto that holy ground
Between wolf and anguished sound?
A champion if one could be found
A champion if one could be found

CHARLES WAYNE CUMBIE

The Flower

Written: November 8, 2015

A beautiful flower beckons
And a small child climbs thru the rumble
Of a fallen city
The child's small hand reaches for the flower
A flower that fearlessly dares to rise up
Against the storm of war
The flower's beauty offered up to the small hand
A sacrifice for hope and joy to return to the land
The flower, God's witness to man
That all who have fallen will rise again

p.s. Poem depicts a true scene from world war II film documentary footage

Arlington

Written: April 18, 2016

Arlington Virginia called today
I picked up to hear what they had to say
No sound, no one trying to tell me anything
Not even scary breathing
Well, I hung up
I said to myself, you know it's not
Every day you get a wake up
From a famous cemetery
I thought, I hope this is not a bad omen
Trying to tell me something
The unknown soldier giving me a ring
But there was only silence, just silence
The kind of quiet silence
That only Arlington can bring
You know, I was a soldier in my day
But not in an Arlington way
I survived to see a new day
No skill involved, just good old dumb luck
Better men than me have passed away
To that wakeup call in Arlington cemetery
Hopefully that unknown soldier
For me will stay that way
There's no need to rush to meet him

CHARLES WAYNE CUMBIE

I've had a brush or two with Mr. Grim
But good luck has helped me escape him
But old Father Time keeps pushing me in Mr. Death's way
And Father Time, when luck's run out
Will be the one that lets him lead me away
So, no more picking up the phone to the silence of the grave
I will hide behind the skirts of Lady Luck
And try my best to delay that day

p.s. Arlington called me up today, but I hung up, cause I did not want to know the unknown soldier's name

Declaration

Written: 2018
Forward: Wake up! Cause here comes a parody, and it's going to hit you, right between the eyes.

When in the course of human events it becomes necessary for one people to dissolve the political bands that connect them to another people, given what the laws of nature and God demands, and compelling the offended group to shout out, "Vote them out, vote them out!" to establish new laws of a decent kind that have respect for mankind. We must hold them bound to these truths that are self-evident that all people are created equal in the eyes of the lord and that their creator has endowed them with unalienable rights. We hold these truths to be self-evident: no man, no nation has the right to be cruel and unusual in their laws and punishments; no man, no nation has the right in any shape or form to steal or kidnap children and babies; no man, no nation has the right to use children as human shields to defend their borders. Colonist broke the law when they said "no" to King George and the war began. They fought and won that war and a Nation was born by and for these truths we hold so dear that no man, no nation can plunder the God given endowment of unalienable rights whose truths we hold self-evident. Does the flag yet stand over a God-fearing land, for equal we will stand but divided we must fall.

p.s. A parody using words from the declaration of Independence. A response to Trump's evil plan to secure the Mexican border.

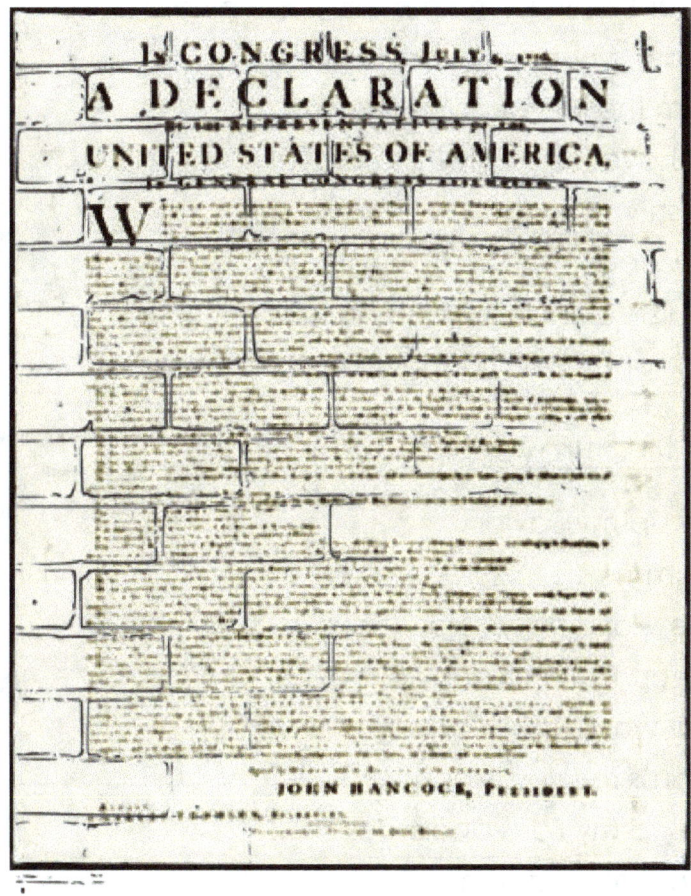

RELIGION

Nothing Left to Give

I asked him,
"Why do your eyes glisten?"
With tears he said,
"I weep for I have nothing more I can give."
Today I saw a hungered one
I gave him the last of my money
Now all I have left to give is a prayer
And a wish you luck
And may God find a way to lighten your way
May you listen and feel, and he will light your way
And the money will no longer be a fish for a day

Answer to a Prayer

(1) Wake up my Savior
    Command the stone away
    The world needs you the most today
(2) Wake up my Lord and say
    The words that can calm
    Man's reckless storm
(3) Wake up my Lord and stay
    The arrogant hand
    We need you more than ever today
    Shine your love and melt man's greed away

CHARLES WAYNE CUMBIE

(4) Wake up my Savior, my Lord, my King
    The world is in great need of your reign
    Let your angels sing your praises
    You who rose and took away death's sting
(5) Wake up my Lord, I want to hear the rocks and stones
    Sing the praises to my King
    Take back thy royal seat and throne
    You've given man his chance to atone
(6) Wake up my lord, start your reign
    No kiss of the ring can save mankind now
    From the mess he's made of things
    Only your love, a love unfeigned
    Can stop the greed of the insane

When the seven signs have run their time
Then and only then will my crown shine
Oh my faithful servant do not despair
Like unto the farmer with patience I tend and care
Watchful waiting for the fruit to bear
For my glory will not be shown
Till the seeds that I have sown are fully grown
Then will I wake up and summon my angels to sing
And bid all mankind to kneel before their king

The Righteous Path

The path you must walk is not an easy one
I have bound your eyes
And you must walk it blind
For only with your heart
Can you see me
The scented breeze
The call of the soaring bird
These can guide you sightless to me
The faith of the heart
Can even in the dark
Bring you unto me
For if you come to me in faith
My path you walk will not forsake
I have sent you prophets with my truth to be told
Like the knotted rope held out for you to hold

Secret Place

Somewhere there's a secret place
I know it's well hidden
Because it's not easily found
But I believe in the place
That it can be found
Some will find it soon
But all will find it late
But sooner or later, It's still a

Wonderful place to see
With faith as the compass and
Belief as the map
You'll find the secret place that's well hidden
And join the lucky ones

Gently the Soft Fall

Soft snowflakes fall on a calm crisp night
Silently they cover all of Earth's scars
Leaving a scene so clean and white
The snowflake blanket quiets all around
The streets lights are crowned in haloed snowflakes glow
As the soft snow settles down in worship of God
Your thoughts rise up to this God
This master artist of it all
Amazed and thankful for this gift of beauty
So freely given quiet without a sound
And like as the snow covers a new world of spotless white
May you be inspired by the sight
And worship your God till your soul is as spotless white

After Life (Son Rise)

Written: Summer, 2010

Just hanging on to my life
One more breath
One more sunrise
My only hope is the promised rise
That the seeds sown in faith
Will grow a new fine day
And with the help of the Word
I'll stand again with strength
And light in my eyes
And create my own sunrise

Beyond Measure

Written: October, 2010

How many times can you look up for guidance from above?
And, have wisdom like manna quietly settle down like a dove.
Then you know...
... you know before you ask.
And with gentle tears of gratitude you long for the feeling to last:
Your thirst quenched

Your hunger fed
Such kindness
Such loving care
And, the answer comes for you to share,
Whispered with a God's breath that vibrates the very soul,
"As many times as you look up to behold."
Know always that you are loved beyond measure,
For your soul is my precious treasure.

Judgement

Written: October 7th, 2010

My God is alive
The prophets call
And, then the stones begin to fall
And sacrilege is the call
Yet, some to their knees do fall
One path
      One word
The chosen call him out by name
And God draws near to save
A world from its shame
Then mankind will know
On that judgement day
It's only they to blame

You Know Not

Written: October, 2010

Man's Judgement:
Why do you take notice of this wretch
So filthy with his sin
How can you love such a one

The Lord explains:
You know not him
You see only the shallow skin
But, I know the depth of him
He may have lost his way
But I know his brave heart
Can be saved this day
I will show him how to drive
His sins away
And he will stand noble once again
And I will count him as my friend

The Lord's message:
For what you cast off I will gather in
For I have purchased away all of their sins
So, it was in the beginning
So, it will be to the end

CHARLES WAYNE CUMBIE

Forgive Us

Written: 2011

Oh Savior of man
I weep at the sight
Of your pierced hand

And even though hate is all we gave
Still, you offered up your life
That we might be saved

We have cursed ourselves
With our hate and our greed
But you have blessed us
With your loving heart and
Promised that we may be freed

May we one day ascend and meet you again
In that sacred sky and be worthy of
Your promise that we will never die

POEMED | RELIGION

Don't Care Anymore

Written: January 11th, 2011

I don't care, I accept what's there, I don't care anymore
You won't get a rise out of me, for I have set all my anger free
No longer to embrace my problems with open arms of care
I turn my back and refuse with them my energy to share

I accept, I accept things as they are
I no longer have a need to settle a score
When the Buddha set under his tree
He became aware
That to accept is to be free
And when Christ hung upon his tree
He showed us
That the only way to be free
Was to accept and forgive
"For they know not what they do"

No score to settle, no spreading the harm
No need for anger or worry or alarm
Just accept and be free
No longer let your worry and anger be a bother
Like the soothing words of the mother
Who tells her child shush, shush; now, it will be alright

CHARLES WAYNE CUMBIE

Let your worries and care take flight
till they're no longer in your sight.

I won't waste my energy keeping up a fight
So if God wants to win back his world
He'll have to use his own might
For I accept it, whatever it will be
And I will seek out my own special tree
And set myself down to be free

Signs of the Times

Written: March 18, 2011

A man stands on the corner
Holding up the sign of the times
"God bless and give if you care"

An old woman begs while shivering
In the rain mixed with snow
Just another sign of the times though

And the signs of the times go up
In front of the empty places
As slowly each town
Its ghost embraces

And sad is our lot for we've
Let the pot get too hot
And, though we complain
We know who's to blame
Greed is his name
A sign of the times
Just more of the same

God sent his son to teach love and compassion
And to our shame, he was held up on a cross

CHARLES WAYNE CUMBIE

Yet another sign of the times

But, at what cost for he had
So much more he could teach us
A higher law of love and divineship
With no eye or tooth to forfeit up
Only the need to drink from the cup
An act of love unmeasured by law
Only kindness and mercy could fill it up
A higher sign of the times

POEMED | RELIGION

Jumping in the Volcano

Written: May 16, 2011

    The Holy man all robed up in his sacredness, preached to the virgins, 'the Gods are angry, you must go to the place that's highest and with your fall you'll save us all, jumping in the volcano'.

    A world away another righteous plea from the ordained is made, 'to save the crops and bring the rain you must unmake what you have made'. So, the priestly order is given, the young daughters would be slayed to soothe the Gods of heaven.

    In yet another worldly place, a sacred order is given, 'to win the favor of heaven, all your possessions must be given; and when there's nothing left to take, you can step to the rim of that holy volcano and jump on in without the fear of the forsaken'.

    The wise man said, 'to save God's children, you must kill God's children'. The young men ask, 'how can this be', and the answer is given, 'be quiet for you must not question the mind of God, sometimes we must jump into the volcano'. But don't worry, the task will be easier if we give the chosen for death an unholy name, and then there will be no shame or need to weep for the slain. So, the followers join in the kill to see how much blood they can spill.

So, beware when the bible thumpers come to town and declare that you must bow down for they have found God's secret message in that ancient passage. Be careful of those who claim God's mind to know or you'll be the next in line to go jumping in the volcano.

p.s. Don't drink the koolaide

The Apology

Written: July 28, 2011

When I was young I felt your love so warm
But I let the feeling grow cold
I took opportunities given
And in my laziness let them slip away
And took my gift of life for granted
I wasted the day
Oh! Such a foolish servant I have been
To not appreciate the hand given
Your love was full with your grace
But I was shallow, undeserving of your embrace
Now the shadows of my life grow long
And the cold settles in my bones
And I can only hope that forgiven I may be
And once again feel the warmth of your love for me

Silent Prayer

Written: August 23, 2011

In prayer I reach as high as I can
To try and touch the mind of God
I try and buy his helping hand with my adoration
But silence is there
I try to beg and plead
To emphasize my need
But silence is there
I promise to follow a truthful path
If only he would grant my wish
And give me what I want to have
But silence is there
Why this silence I ask
Have I not given you offerings
And service when I can
All I'm asking for is a helping hand
But silence is there
Desperate in my sadness
I turn away feeling forsaken and
Lost as I go my way
The heavens are closed it seems
But then it dawns on me that there
Might be one more thing to say
"Father forgive me for I have lost my way
What can I do to show my love for you today?"
And, then noise is so loud

I'm driven prostrate to the ground
A Chorus of angels singing round and round
A joyful song about a helpful hand
My hand held out to my fellow man

Silent Prayer (Short Version)

Written: August 23, 2011

In prayer I reach out to touch God's mind
To buy his helping hand with adoration
But silence is there
I beg and plead to emphasize my need
But silence is there
I promise a truthful path
If he would give what I would have
But silence is there
Why silence I ask? Have I not given
Offerings and service when I can
But silence is there
In sadness I turn away
Forsaken as I go my way
Might there yet be one more thing to say?
Father forgive me for I have lost my way
What can I do to show my love for you today?
The noise, it's so loud I'm driven to the ground
A chorus of angels singing round and round
A joyful song of a helpful hand
My hand held out to my fellow man

He's in the Book (of Life)

Written: September, 2011

If they write about him
If they write at all
I hope they say that he cared
He cared about it all
He did what he could when others should
He could not walk away from those
With eyes that pled to be fed
Those who had more could not be found
So, he gave what he could
To those who sat on the ground
In that book, write it down
That he was one that
Could be found

After thoughts:
Excuses:
I gave at the office; Get a job; probably spend it on booze; too lazy to work; I give to the church not faceless bums

CHARLES WAYNE CUMBIE

When Rocks and Stones Begin to Sing

Written: November 1, 2011

I want to be there when the rocks and stones begin to sing
The long wait over as everlasting peace descends among man
When kindness is the only tender that's held dear
The beat of love's heart the only score to keep
We'll stand hand in hand all relieved
As what we believed, now all can see
As hatreds mask is pulled away
The day of man is past
Like puddles that cannot last
In the brightness of the day

The Righteous Rich

Written: September 3, 2011
About: What would happen if God decided to make one of his own a member of the righteous rich?

A new richman stands on the corner and sees all ….

Bread lines and beggar signs
No medicines or nurses for those with empty purses
A little boy with only a stick for a toy
The little girl with dirty hair no hope for a curl
Those turned away into a sleepless night cause the shelter is full

God's richman looks at this piteous sight
Raises his eyes to the sky and Pleads for their plight
You gave us your word
That a fish for a day is the lesser way
Teach to fish is how to save the day

So, God inspires
And the man knows what he requires

A factory is built
And those forsaken by country
Are welcomed in

CHARLES WAYNE CUMBIE

The door is shut
And the fences go up
Keeping out that bottom line
With all that the market can bare

For God has raised up
Someone to care
In all the profits, now
The people will share

And as factories go up across the land
The workers leave the lesser man
And take their labor where they can stand
No longer the economic slave
And, in time by God's hand
The country is saved

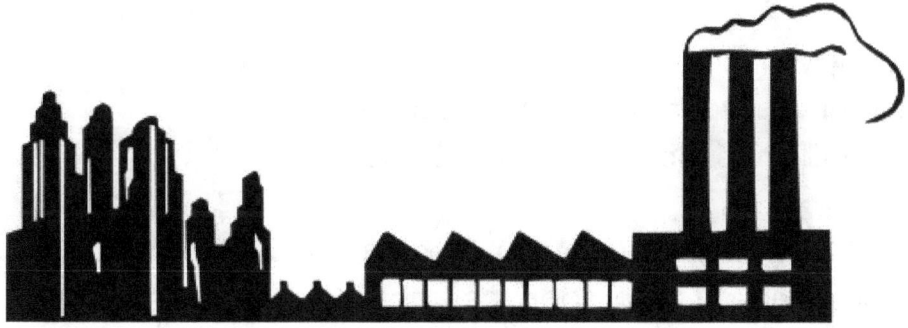

God's Conversation with an Inventor

Written: February 10, 2012 at midnight on a Friday

My sand has almost run out
Now with so little, what can I do?

Your path does not end here
You will finish what you start
Even though your sand has run out

Then what best should I start
If the finish must be a bridge a part?

Think service to your fellow man
It's the only deed that will stand

What talent do I have that can
Serve at such late date?

Apply your heart and I will inspire
Your inventive mind soon will acquire
The brilliance that can win the desire

And what might be a worthy desire
Whose service might span the gap
Between this path and that?

Be it helpful to the injured, poor, and aged

The relief of sufferings will be its test
And then you'll know your choice was best

So, I shall give thought to what deed might be brought to share,
To what talents I may have and wait with thoughtful stare
To be made aware of what can be brought forth
To satisfy the test, whose help will be the best

Looking Up

Written: 2012

When you find that you've hit bottom
All that's left is looking up
Life can be so tough
That you feel you've had enough
Then all that's left is looking up
And when your fears give you a scare
And you think there's no one to care
Then all that's left is looking up
If you do it with a prayer
You just might find there's someone there
That man who owns it all
Know that he has seen your fall
And there is no shame, no shame at all
If on his name, you do call

Heaven's Gate

Written: 2012

Oh, woman!
Heaven's gate
Usherer of Earth's souls
You raise them up unto
their fate
God's favored of all
Only you
With your push can
immortals fall
And, it will take a God's
forgiveness
To save them
If they can be saved at all

CHARLES WAYNE CUMBIE

The Ohmn of the Didge

Written: May, 2012

Someday I just might
Strike that God's note
Me and my tubes vibrations
The one he used for creation
That will be the day
I transcend without ever
Opening death's door
And all you'll find of me
Is my tube on the floor
The God meditation of
The tubes vibration
So come and give a listen
To see if I can summon God near
Just tube and me in deep communion
Summoning the Godly union

A Better Way

Written: June 3, 2012

There's a better way
Look to the son
Listen to what he has to say
His word will save
And show a better way
No more greed or hunger
There's a better way
Hear what the son has to say
No more unkind words or
Hate filled blows
Or feeling so smart you look
Down your nose
There is a better way
The son's word shows
The kindness love bestows
So, as your tears wet your face
And it is your grief you must embrace
There is a better way
Drink from his word and you will
Thirst no more, for as he was lifted
So will be the burdens that you bore
Love, his love, it is the better way

CHARLES WAYNE CUMBIE

Will God Make it Right

Written: December 6, 2012

Will God make it right
Well I don't know
But he said he would
Bad forgiven
Lost brought home
His love shown
The price paid

Will God make it right
Well I don't know
But he said he would
All the loved ones
That he made
Freed from tomb and grave
No more wounded, hurt, or afraid
A just God's will to make it right
And love the sadness away

Will God make it right
Well I don't know
But he said he would

Care of the World

Written: September 10, 2013

When there's sadness in your eyes
And nothing you do can make it otherwise
Just know that this world is made of dust
And to dust it surely will crumble
And any, and all of trouble
That brings sadness to your eye
Will fade like the dust on the wind
For God's plan for you is happiness
And sadness cannot win

As you grow older, the things thought so important
Life's worries, and cares seem more like a fool's errand
With wizened eye you realize, the cares of the world
Slip through the fingers like sand
And back to the dust they go (again)
For God's plan is happiness for you
Against this nothing of this world can stand

CHARLES WAYNE CUMBIE

Can God be Surprised?

Written: September 29, 2013

What would it take to make God shout out "Yes!"
Cause God must have seen it all many times before
If I could give him a surprise performance
Might I get a standing ovation
But this begs the question
Can god be surprised?
Answer that one and you'll be standing with the wise
Is God just a good guesser
Or does he use fate to contrive?
Can he see ahead to every move
You will make while you're alive?
It's not a thing that man can know
Do I wear concrete shoes and to the depths I must go
Or can I go anywhere I want to go?

Worship

Written: May, 2014

If I danced in the rain
Would you call me insane
And if I wasted my hours
Searching for the sun
Would you shake your head
At what I have done
Oh, my soul aches for its freedom
As I pray for a kingdom given
And the prophets all say
There'll be a better day
Do you mind if I wait for it
By this beautiful bay
Admiring God's gift of beauty
No longer the slave to duty
Just a soul worshiping a silent God
But, his beauty shouts out like a song
He took a bit of nothing
And made something
So beautiful, as the woman I love

CHARLES WAYNE CUMBIE

God's People

Written: June 23, 2014

Happy people stay happy
Loving people please stay loving
Selfless people keep sharing
Helpful people please keep helping
Friendly people keep on befriending
Cause you are the ones
That keep this world sound
Make it worth staying around
Your names will be written down
Not in the book of the dead
But in the glorious book of life
You are the ones that save this
World from its condemnation
And when the heavens look down
And gaze upon every nation
You'll know that you will be found
Standing on the higher ground
And your reward, a righteous crown

A Prayer

Written: October 18, 2014

Dear Father,

God of all creation
I thank you for my salvation
And for the love you have for all your
Sons and daughters of every nation
You have shown us the way
A brightly lit path that to the soul beckons
And now all one need do is listen
To the voice of a loving God
Who with open arms calls out
"Come unto me and I'll place your
Hand on the iron rod
And you will not fall or stumble"
As long as you keep humble
And the Holy Spirit will keep you safe
From all trouble
Feel its power to turn your face into the light
So that you might always know what is right
Thank you Father for you have
Sent your son, the word, the power of resurrection
That all might stand and be made whole again
Forgiven

CHARLES WAYNE CUMBIE

So they say drink from the cup of life and
Fulfil the promise given
That man is that he may have joy
A gift from a loving God in heaven
Amen

A Prayer Extra Verse:
Thank you for this life's test
That I might learn to be my best
To learn the loving kindness
That you hold so dear
That I might grow
Worthy to draw near
And bask in the presence
Of your wondrous love
What kinder father can there be
Whoever strives to set us free
From all the heavy burdens of sins
That hold us down
Keeping us from
That promised crown

Oh! Father so worthy of prayer
You are the champion who stands between
Us and Death's door

POEMED | RELIGION

Dawn (The Watcher)

Written: October 30, 2014

I watch with a yawn
As the quiet dawn
Moves slowly through the trees
Golden beams bright
Warming the world with light
Mother nature wakes and unfurls its leaves
Her creatures come alive
Rising up from where they lie
To welcome the coming day
The beauty of it all
Makes me want to fall
To my knees and worship
This God of beauty
Master artist of it all
Such a worthy God
Who creates scenes that render
Such golden splendor
I watch as the dew jeweled world
Seems to turn and smile at me
I stand and smile back
And shake my head at the sight
Of this impossible beauty
What a wonderful, wonderful thing

To be alive to see
This scene, this dream
That only the supreme being
Could conjure up

God Among Us

Written: December 15, 2014

Today a child is born among us
A God to walk among men
With mercy in his hands
A savior and a friend
He speaks with love the words of wisdom
Guiding those who kneel and listen
Onto the path of redemption
The gift of life he offers
And through him all will be born anew
To a life without threat or contention
He silently beckons with a whisper
To the soul, "come unto me and be made whole"
All creation recognizing the voice
of the word first spoken
When the darkness was broken
And the first eye opened
Waits to eagerly obey
His righteous command
Over all the land

Getting High

Written: December 19, 2014

As my days grow more and more weary
I go down to that ocean shore
And look out on its waves of soft green
My eyes rise above to the blue cloudless sky
I see gulls floating on air as they sail bye
And in my mind's eye, I set myself free
To be there, where I can meet them eye to eye
And together we look down upon the Earth
Where all my cares and troubles be
Finally my mind released and free
Floats gently on the ocean breeze
And I can see as far as eye can see
I fly higher than feathered wing can take
And higher still, till I can feel
Again the proof I need to make
The touch of the maker's hand
And I come to understand that he
Is my truest friend
Loving me unconditionally
Hoping for me to follow
Even higher and be free

CHARLES WAYNE CUMBIE

A Bridge to Nowhere

Written: 2015

Every thought you've had I've thought
Every idea you've dreamed I've dreamed before you
I built the stage you conduct your acts of brilliance on
Like the tower of Babel, you build a bridge to nowhere
All your science, all your educated guesses
Cannot get you off this bridge to nowhere
Take my hand and you won't need a bridge
You can fly or just be there

Kindness is the First Fruit

Written: February 4, 2015

When I finally made it to the highest point, I found him: the ancient one. He was old now. He had studied the heavens all his life. I asked him, "What does God want most from us?" He said, "To be worshipped."
"And how do I worship him?" I asked.
The ancient one answered, "With kindness. God wants to teach you love and kindness is the first fruit to come from love true. Kindness strews the path of love with perfumed petals that fall as soft as dove's wings; more binding than any golden ring. It's with your acts of kindness that you worship him, our Lord and King."

Ghost

Written: December 23, 2014

Do you believe in ghosts?
Some say yes and some say no
But there is one I know
A Ghost that won't be denied
For when he's sent for you
He will be recognized
All truths revealed, no chance for a lie
No way to get it wrong
No place to hide
He gives a feeling so strong
You'll feel it in your bones
And the light within that was so dim
Will grow strong and burn bright again
So yes, I believe in this Ghost
He is the Ghost who removes all doubt
And once he strikes home
You'll want to shout out
And tell everyone what you've found out
That now you understand
That there is a grand plan
And of the triad God of all man
The Holy Ghost is the one
To remove all doubt and reveal the plan

p.s. As I see it
God, the father, provides the plan
The Holy Ghost reveals the plan
Jesus, the word, carries out the plan

They Prayed

Written: April 8, 2015

Once there was a child who was afraid
    So he prayed
Once there was a mother who was afraid
    So she prayed
Once there was a soldier who was afraid
    So he prayed
Once there was a boat full of fishers of men
Who were afraid
    So they prayed
Once a loved one wrapped in a shroud
Entombed was laid
    So the savior prayed
        And he came forth from the grave
Once there was a day when death
Had the final say
But once the stone rolled away
On that Easter day
It was the Lord who had
    The final say

God's Witness/Choose a Gift

Written: February 8, 2015
About: Compilation of two poems

If I could choose a gift it would be
Compassion and kindness
To be my driving force
A life gifting out to others
Sharing a love like a child's for its mother
Each day a quest to bring for awhile
A much needed smile
To care enough to share
To heal the blank stare
Of life's travelers left on the side of the road
Waiting for some stranger's kindness to be bestowed
Their signs call out
But no artist hand held the pen
The stroke was made from a desperate need
For help to be given
As you go bye
With ignoring eye
Think not that all is forgiven
For these, the least of these
Are man's gage and the mark is made in heaven

CHARLES WAYNE CUMBIE

You Only Have to Believe

Written: April 17, 2015

You have to believe
    Like the stone believed
    When it was moved by the angels hand
    And the Light of life came streaming out
You have to believe
    Like the blind man
    Who sitting in his darkness
    Felt the touch that brought back the sky
You have to believe
    Like the waters did when they heard the sound
    That parted them to dry ground
You have to believe
    Like the shepherds and the wise men
    Who saw the Light come down
    And the Omega King was found
You have to believe
    Like the dove believes that
    On feathered wing
    It will be lifted up by the unseen
You have to believe
    Like the small child, reaching for a flower
    In the rubble of a war-torn city
    Believes in a world that still has beauty
You only have to believe

In God We Trust

Written: March 3, 2015

When His spirit moves you
You know, you will just know
No test tube show
Can prove it though
But the need is there
The need to know
For without the Father
There can be no son, no daughter
No future, no hope
When the lights go out you are
Left with no place to go
All is lost, such an unforgivable cost
The grave becomes your new master, your lonesome God
A warden whose chains won't ever let go
And when the worm turns, it turns on you
You can lead the student life
Studying the book of life or book of dead
But knowledge of the page
Or that of the sage
Can't shield you from the unknown
Both paths lead to a dark age
Only with faith can the light be shown
And the believer's path be known
The scientist cannot escape
That faith is the final equation he can't break

CHARLES WAYNE CUMBIE

For it takes as much faith to deny the deity
As that of the sage to confirm it
Faith is all that mankind has
Be it God or the tube
Only when you can no longer bleed
Will the truth be known to you
The scientist puts his faith in the page
Each page a grain of sand always
Shifting in the wind
A house built on quicksand
And fall it must for time it can't stand
For this test, this timeless rock
Is God's domain where his truth
Remains the same
To put your faith in man is to build your house on sand
In God we trust
Is the purest mettle that will not rust
The atheist puts his faith in man
The agnostic knows not where to stand
Neither has a plan that does not shift with the sand
Why pay the cost of life with copper when you can use gold
Be careful to not let science or religion
Like the blinders on the mule
Tunnel your vision
The believer puts his faith in the Master's hand
That conducts the better celestial plan

p.s. Written for those who don't know what they know

A Promise Given

Written: May 12, 2015

There is a promise given
That there is something more
All you have to do
Is knock on that door
And you will receive
What you believe
You know the deceiver
He will deceive
And the doubter
He will doubt
But there is a way
That you can find out
You just have to
Knock on that door
When the prayer is true
It can get through
And will be heard like
A knock on the door
And then your eyes will be opened
To something more

To Plead

Written: October, 2015

I feel the need to plead for the man who has lost his soul; to plead with golden words that might shake from the heavens a rain of forgiveness that the man might fill his cup with the nectar of life, and drink the cure to remove the blight that darkens his soul and blinds his sight; to plead for the man that he might with opened eye gaze through the portal of righteous Light and awaken his cloaked mind to the truth of his immortal life, and know the thrill of life that there will be an end to the night and the sun will shine again on his future, like the newborn's sight.

Tough Love

Written: May 20, 2015

So, all knowing one
What was that flood all about?
Did you get surprised by a flurry of doubt?
They say it's insane
Expecting different results while doing the same
Did I hear you right
That next time it will be fire to set things right
I'm sure you're warming up a lightning bolt even as I speak
But this is tough love
And you need to hear this from
Someone you created in your image
Even though they may be weak
Did you create in your image
Because you needed to look at yourself more often
Or were you shooting for someone to talk to
Well, this is tough love and it's time to listen up
You can't keep blaming the lab rats
When your experiments go belly up
For those of you who may be worried
About the words of this poem or how I've spoke
Don't, for I must admit, no one can know the mind of God
No matter how much the need or want
He can't be disturbed or woke

CHARLES WAYNE CUMBIE

So, forgive me for how I've spoke
But, careful now when you hear this poem
Don't stand to close
Especially if out loud it's read
He's warming up his lightning bolt
And you could end up dead

p.s. What? You want to stone me

p.p.s. Post log parody of a Bill Cosby joke
Hey, that's the darkest cloud I think I've ever seen
And it looks like it's starting to rain
It's not a flood is it?
Ok, lord it's just you and me right
No hard feelings, right?

Evolution Solution

Written: August 1, 2015

For eons, time stirred the pot
And Light became the building block
Evolution that lucky chance
Turned Light into a living dance
The blocks were laid
And life was finally made
Only the best designs in elimination time
Were left for the future outline
And from this evolutionary tide
A new form was born
And the slow ebb that stirred the pot
Bowed out to an intelligent guide
From the top of the evolutionary chain
A new creator came
That held the designer gene
And then intelligent design
became the new more efficient way
And to the building blocks
His spirit of intelligence he did add
And the spirit became the scaffold for the flesh
And the first begot was got
The makers breed began to breathe
And the universe became a living breathing thing
There was no more need for a mold
For the spirit did what it was told
The spirit of awareness had taken hold
And all creation recognized its maker
A new alpha God to behold

CHARLES WAYNE CUMBIE

So you see,
Evolution had already fulfilled its plan
Even before Earth received a man
And the evolution solution
Was finally brought to fruition
And a new supreme being was formed
You say, evolution is the only way
Then in a way man is proof of the
Evolution solution, for evolved he is
Into an intelligent designer, but in infancy
Given time he may be a God of design
And evolution having finished its job
Must bow out to the more efficient way
No more eons of stirring the pot

p.s. Evolution by its own theory predicts the coming of a supreme designer

p.p.s. Here's an added twist of thought for all you deep thinkers... a supreme being could easily be a master of time. So, evolution with the added attraction of intelligent design could happen in the twinkling of an eye; seven days or seven eons, makes no difference to the master of time.

p.p.p.s So now the evolutionist and the diest non-believer and believer can hold hands and watch the final sunset as the stars fade and take all existence away.

Choose Wisely

Written: December 14, 2015

What words can be said
That would make you believe
In both the living and the dead
Will you go where you are led
Like lemmings to the ledge
Falling to oblivion's darkness
Or will you choose instead
To fall to your knees in worship of the Light
Know that in the Light there is love for you
And from the tree of life you will be fed
And the living will hold hands with the dead
How can I make these words impress
That you might be among the blessed
And free from death's rest
Two choices there are that can be made
One to the creator and one to the grave

CHARLES WAYNE CUMBIE

After Life (The Question)

Written: December 5, 2016

The most important question ever asked
The most important question that will ever be asked
Is there an afterlife?
Answer this and you'll be standing with the wise
Answer it with life
And you have hope
Answer it with death
And all you have is despair
Pray for hope, without it
All that's gone before is just that, gone
No sound without the ear
No light without the eye
No hope without the soul
Pray hard, the hardest you've ever prayed
For hope
Pray for hope
And may the afterlife
Welcome you with sunshine

POEMED | RELIGION

For the Love of God

Written: September 7, 2016
Dedication: A poem for my God
About: David would sing and it pleased the lord, may this poem please

Part 1: Prodigal Soul Speaks
The beauty of sky and Earth, that was you
Commanding the poetic thought
To come forth and be
Seven sounds echoing the poemed thought
And from the dark the spin of life was brought
That spirit glue that's in the world thru and thru
You created the beautiful sky
For your return from a long goodbye
And the Earth for our practice home
Oh! How beautiful this Earth and sky
So pleasing to the mortal eye
The sights, the sounds, and feel
Though it be practice, it's so real
You sent us your Son to teach a higher law
The merciful forgiveness for flaw
Even the doubting-Thomas's of all races
Are shown the way to cross that bridge of
Righteousness into the arms of their loved one's embraces
Thank you for the way you saved us all

CHARLES WAYNE CUMBIE

From that Angel's fall
Love and forgiveness closing the door
On the eye for eye and picking at the sore
May it be that someday I will see
You again face to face
For behind the stone was empty space
And walk again with you in our true home

<u>Part 2: The Father Speaks</u>
I delight in the happiness and joy
Of my children when they at last
Step into the light
When the sun beckons you awake do your eyes not open?
When the door opens do you not step thru?
When the road is clear do you not cross over?
Let your spirit awaken
Knock and let the door open
The road is mapped clear
Go ahead, cross that righteous bridge
Your true home awaits you
My prodigal spirit child I have missed you
Come unto me, you need not be on your own
And receive your inheritance, your true home

A Simple Thought

Written: June 17, 2017

I may not be able to stop the
World from spinning
But maybe there's a way to stop the
World from sinning
It's easy to know his game
You can see it right there in the biblical pages
Throughout the ages it's always been the same
I decided to counter punch his bad with good
To make sure he understood
That I was onto his sinister ways
Cause every time he tried to make me sad
Or influence the bad
He instead was the one that was had
I would turn his lemons into sweet lemonade
When his influence threw trouble in my path
When something would happen that was bad
He expected me to be upset, angry, and to lash out
In kind but instead I find a way to balance
The scales tipped his way I would go out
Of my way to do something good for something bad
Something good to make him mad
For I, with this simple thought and action
Had stopped his spread of sinful reaction
To return a blow with a caress is hard to do
But it is the best

CHARLES WAYNE CUMBIE

No building of polished wood
Or gold inlays needed
No steeple standing over the people
No pews or dues to be had
Although I understand the command
Of one day a week in the church they meet
But the church I speak of it has no
Walls to confine, no name, no sign
The world is my congregation and to them
My actions are the words I preach
There is no one day limit
For my world's congregation
I balance the scales with a simple compensation
Righting a wrong with a right
When it catches on will win the fight
And mad he will be with his influence weakened
And that my friend is how we should keep him
If you haven't guessed yet
I speak of satan
He is the prince of mean
Make each punch he throws
Turn into a ripple of good to soothe the injury
And the fight can be won, that's how it's done
So, hold on tight to this simple thought
And cure the world's pain with a caress

POEMED | RELIGION

Death's Sting

Written: June 19, 2017

I am the prince of this world
Your God has given you to me
And I will ensnare you, you'll never be free
Outcast though I be, but I'll make sure
I bring you down with me
Not even a hurricane of doves can save thee
As you look to the heavens, I set at your feet
A gaping hole to trip thee
For you see, I am your test
And I don't grade on a curve
You will rise or fall on your own,
You'll get what you deserve
The tests, the trials, the doubts will go on and on
A long time, till the last breath, till your
Dying breath and then you'll be
Mine, mine, mine
Even the great David
Could not hold against my tests
No matter how sweet his song
He did not rise, his bones are still here in the dust
So, what chance have you, such a common lessor thing
No chance at all so
Sing, sing, sing

CHARLES WAYNE CUMBIE

To your savior the king
Tell him he'll have to send more than doves
To take back your soul
So, yesss… death will
Sting, sting, sting

p.s. Don't worry I was just trying to get into the mind of Satan, but not to stay there

Oh! God Where Are You?

Written: September 25, 2017

Oh! God where are you?
There, in the blue sky held up by the tree topped hills
Oh! God where are you?
There, in the angel face of the sleeping child
Oh! God where are you?
There, in the soothing touch of the sisters hand
Oh! God where are you?
There, in the cool water held to the dry lips
Oh! God where are you?
There, in the artist eye, skilled ready to reveal
Oh! God where are you?
There, in the inner voice that troubles the heart
Oh! God where are you?
There, giving peace where there's despair
Oh! God where are you?
There, in the herald angels song of the second coming
Oh! God where are you?
Up there, winning mercy for the likes of me
Oh! God where are you?
I love you, thank you, thank you

Happily Ever After

Written: February 22, 2018

(God)
> How can you have happily ever after
> There can be a happily ever after

(My Lord)
> When the sunrise meets the sunset
> There's the happily ever after
> When the storm breaks into the dawn
> There's the happily ever after
> When the babes cry turns to laughter in the mother's arms

(The Father)
> There's the happily ever after of the Father
> When the knowing brings that understanding love
> There's the happily ever after of the Father

(The Son)
> When the forgiving kiss heals the wounded heart
> There's the happily ever after
> When justice bows before many
> There's the happily ever after

(God the Father, the Son, and the Holy Ghost)
> Father into thy loving arms I command my spirit
> Therein lies the happily ever after

POEMED | RELIGION

Ode to My Lord

Written: December 12, 2018
About: On the 12th of December 2018, my doctor told me my PSA was at zero and decided to keep me on hormone therapy for 2 years to be on the safe side of things.

Hurray for the bright new day
Hurray for the stay
Of the executioner's hand
I won't be going into the dark just yet
Two years free to feel the sunshine
On my face
Fresh air to breathe
There's been a two-year reprieve!
Thank you, Lord, for the blessing I've received
And a thank you to the many angels praying
Oh! There's joy to all, for with the love of our King
We are saved from the fall
There are poems to write and songs to sing
There are flowers to be seen
Shiny in the gentle rain
My soul is afloat as I write the poems
And sing the songs to praise my King
It's with the song of life I now sing
"On the twelfth day of Christmas
The good Lord gave to me

CHARLES WAYNE CUMBIE

One free pass, let's hope it lasts
With no creature stirring inside
No place for it to hide or reside
It's a life-giving hormone...ney
May God's will be done
And songs of praise to him be sung
Thank you, Lord, for the blessing
A shiny new spark begins to glow"

REFLECTIONS

Echoes of the Past

When the echoes of sadness haunt your past
And the future slips away so fast that
It makes you regret that nothing lasts
So, soon your future becomes lost in the past

Too Much

Sometimes life is too much
It comes at you with crushing blows
But there is no shame if you cry in the rain
Cause anyone looking can't see a thing
Sometimes life is too much
It drives you down
And each time it's harder to get up
Someday I'll go down and stay down
And all that will be left of me
Is a chalk line on the ground

CHARLES WAYNE CUMBIE

I Name You

When, where, how?
Is it the beginning
Or is it the end?
Hope brings the beginning
Despair brings the end
If the eye never sees the light
Then why the stars?
Will you accept the gifts I bring
The gifts I give you?
When the name was given
Was spoken
Who named you
Named you with power

Calm

Written: December 8, 2010

I need to go somewhere new and stop
Stand in sunshine on some coastline
Stroll the docks to soothe my soul
Seek out nature's friends

The ant found, sharing his walk with me
I try to see what he's about
In his silent world undisturbed
By even a shout
I watch him follow an unseen path
Heading back for home

As I seek that elusive calm
My eyes look up to that blue sky
I marvel at the skillfulness of a seagull who sits on air
As if holding its breath to make a decision
So, as the gull has taught, I still my mind as I walk
No need for any thought
Just a calm like still waters
And in its mirror of stillness
Your face I see

CHARLES WAYNE CUMBIE

The time has come to leave sand and sea
And like the ant find my path
Back home to you and family

Dead Thoughts

Written: August, 2011

I'm walking the streets of the past in my head
Counting up my dead
Life's blood has long for them been bled
Now they're only memories in my head
On hope we've all been fed
To believe no such thing as the dead
There is no good and gone for us to long
We'll see them again face to face
In some holier place
So, there's no need to waste our time
Fretting about life's deadline
All that we've ever known
All that we'll ever know
Is hidden behind death's door
Far away on heavens distant shore

The Lost and Found

Written: January 6, 2012

I look out from what's my universe
And contemplate the human curse
With weary thoughts, I try to remember
Those things taught, I'm lost in the why
So to find myself I ask the dreary questions
Is there no help for what's lost
No path to lead
Or apple seed to mark the trail
Someone to live to tell the tale
When the compass is broken
What then do you do
What magic words must be spoken
To conjure the tunnels light
So easy for one to lose sight
When there is but dimmed light
Is my lost and found held captive
By the one who stands on higher ground
All glory and claim to fame to be
Offered up in humble apology
Must I go into the coldness of the night
Not even glowing ember left
To show there was a life

p.s.
Aztecs say 2012 is the apocalypse day
Maybe I should write a warding poem
To wish it all away

Despair

Written: December 20, 2012

How do I find the familiar shore
How can I get to the unlocked door
There is a sadness locked inside me
I know not how to set it free
It's like a shadow that follows
Unshakeable, unfleeable
Even in the bright sun
Still it clings to me
Saddens and chills the soul
How do I find even a single light
That will lift from me this unforgiving blight
As I stare and look about
I cannot find the route
That can guide me through this
Mapless night
I still can see no way that I might
Get near the familiar shore or
That unlocked door

To Cry Alone

Written: January 20, 2013
Dedication: This poem is dedicated to Karise Eden, who's voice inspired it

Today I heard a voice that made me cry
With tears that would not dry
From a heartfelt soulful bleed
You could feel the longing and the need
And you just knew you had found someone else
Who cried alone
A voice that makes you feel the pain
When you just know life's left you standing in the rain
To cry alone
Oh, that voice will make you feel
All the sadness that's your own
And then you'll know there's someone else
Who cries alone
The song was a soothing salve
But the voice was a friend to have
And together we cried alone

CHARLES WAYNE CUMBIE

The Other Side of Town

Written: February, 2013

They say any day above ground is a good day
But I don't know
They also say it's better on the other side of town
If you look my way you might catch a frown
Because I don't know if it's above
Or the other side I should be found

Together Again

Written: May, 2013

Will I see you again in that forgotten sky?
When sin did blind my eye and faith took wing to fly
May I once again see that forgotten sky
Two paths of life I've had to try:
One mapped with faith, the other paved with fear
Tears of joy or tears of sorrow
The path I chose will be my tomorrow
May I once again see that forgotten sky
May there be tears of joy for that tomorrow

Spring

Written: March 16, 2014
Spring, spring, spring!
The beautiful weather
Does put a spring in one's step doesn't it
The glistening new growth, all clean and wet
Life comes to life
No more huddles in warm places
Now it's wonderful flowers
And the whites and pinks of the trees
It's out into the golden sun
Out into the open spaces
Breathing in the perfumed breeze
As death in winter goes cold
Life in the spring grows warm
Love as they say is in the air
Birds chirping, nesting
Once again in the park
Is a place for resting
Enjoying the beauty of the nature's trees
The humming birds and bees
Visiting the awakened flowers
Gentle sun warmed showers
Children playing with their laughter and their tease
It's wonderful, wonderful to see
Just to be the observer

CHARLES WAYNE CUMBIE

The sights the sounds
The birds that hover
It's life
Life given
And life worth liven

POEMED | RELIGION

Some of Me (Sorry for the Bragg)

Written: March 18, 2014

Careful, get too close
You'll step into the minefield of my mind
What you think you know about me
Will come apart if you take me too lightly
It's a world event to see through me
Out of the box is where I'll be
You won't need my life's map
To find where I am at
I'm right here in the dream
The scientific dream
And though I might seem
To not have a scheme
Who knows what or where you
Might find me
Can you guess the what is next
It's a dreamer's way to play
Come step onto my field of dreams
You might find the magic
That directs the play
And if you take
My dreams to heart
Who knows, like Einstein
They might just take
Your world apart

CHARLES WAYNE CUMBIE

A Spring Day Walk

Written: April 11, 2014
About: Composed on a walk in the sunshine of a spring day

I think it's going to be
A sun shiny day
Looks like the sun has
Come out just for me
Now, it's official
I'm a retiree
The check's in the mail
And it's just for me
All my days now are free
I take a walk
Whenever I please
Watch the wind wave
Through the trees
It may be invisible to see
But when it touches me
It makes me feel free
The wind goes where it wants
Where it needs to be
We are kindred spirits now
Cause we're both free
And when I see it wave our flag
I know it waves at me
Because it knows
That I'm just as free

POEMED | RELIGION

The Boy and the Kite

Written: July 23, 2014
Dedication: A story poem for Elijah, my grandson

Once there was a boy who wanted a kite, but not just any kite, he wanted a friendly kite with lots of kite string. So, the boy worked hard to make his kite: stick, paper, and glue. And soon, he was out the door and into the field and his kite flew high up in the sky. Up high where the birds fly. But as he looked up and saw his kite, he felt that something wasn't quite right. So, he brought the kite back down to the ground, and with a thoughtful frown, an idea came round. He went back into his house, laid the kite back down and drew a smiley face, nice and round. So, his kite always had a smile for him. Now, at last his kite was just right and from then on it would always be a happy flight.

The boy flew his kite high in the sky every day, but one day as he and his kite were out to play, he ran and ran as fast as he could to make his kite fly very, very high, but suddenly the ground gave way and ruined his kite flying day. He had fallen into an old dry well, but as he fell, tightly he held to his kite string and the kite stayed with him smiling down from the sky. The boy could not get out of the deep dry well, and after a while he worried that he might not get home and would miss his supper cause there was no one to see and no one to tell he was lost out of sight in the deep dry well. He worried that it might get dark and he would have to spend the night, just him and his smiling kite. His family was worried too, it was getting late; so, in search they went for the boy and his kite. After a while, with no luck and no boy in sight, the boy's dad was starting to get sad. When he looked up in the sky he let out a cry cause there was the kite smiling down. The family followed the string that led to the well in the ground, and there was much joy for they had saved the boy and he had made it home in time to be fed. The boy thanked his smiling kite for saving him from spending the night in the deep dry well.

Just A Soul

Written: October, 2014

If I danced in the rain
Would you call me insane
And if I wasted my hours
Searching for the sun
Would you shake you head
At what I have done
Oh, my soul aches for its freedom
As I pray for that promised kingdom
And the prophets all say
There will be a better day
Do you mind if I wait for it
By this beautiful bay
Admiring God's gift of beauty
No longer a slave to duty
Just a soul worshiping a silent God
But his beauty shouts out
Like a song
He took a bit of nothing
And made something .... Beautiful
As beautiful as the woman I love

CHARLES WAYNE CUMBIE

Wagon Maker

Written: May 13, 2016

When looking back on my days
Tell them I lived the ways
Of my name sake Wayne "the wagon maker"
Using tools sometimes almost like
An artist uses the brush
Using only vision's blueprint
Filling the need to express and create
The things of the day to last and stay
Embracing the urge to try and do
Strengthening the weaker design
Till you may find
It holds against the years
And stands a testament
To the artist gone
An artistic life shown
With the simple tools
That can build a home

The Pool

Written: August 5, 2015

The traveler walked
Along the water's edge
And caught sight of a gentle pool

It's so lovely here
So peaceful here
I think I'll rest a while
And admire this pool with water
As clear as a dew drop tear

And as I set beneath the shady tree
Whose limbs droop low as if to show
It had found a new friend to shield
From the sun's hot glow

It's so cool here, it's easy to smile
As I rest and contemplate for a while
The insects have not discovered me yet
So, I can set and enjoy the cool and wet

On this sunny summer's day
Fit only for rest or play
As I relax and take comfort
From this beautiful place

CHARLES WAYNE CUMBIE

It makes it seem so easy to dream
And even contemplate what
God's thought might have been
When he began to paint with his brush
The scene I'm in

So, now I must with much regret
Rise up to go for dusk has come
And the sun will set

And do as all travelers must do
Move on ahead and trek anew
To leave behind this place of rest

But life's memory of it will never fade
Which proves it is the best
Of any place my heart has laid

POEMED | RELIGION

Luck is all you got

Written: October 24, 2018 (my birthday)
About: Written while sitting in the radiation lobby, awaiting my turn

Shiny cars and gold bars
Don't mean a lot when you're standing
In front of that radiation door
Might as well give it all away
And hope it's enough to buy
A spot on that golden shore
It's a scary time when the noose tightens
And the knife is dull
No plans can be made, 'cause it's out
Of your hands
When lady luck is all you've got
Between you and an early date
With the cemetery plot

What Ya Gonna Do

Written: October 25, 2018
About: Inspired by part of a line in the song "Bad Boys Reply"

What you gonna do when they come for you
Cry!

CHARLES WAYNE CUMBIE

Yell Why?
What should you do
What shall you do
What could you do
Cry!
Yell Why?
There is no magic wand
That can be waived
To save you
So, what you gonna do
When they come for you
Cry!
Yell Why?
Hope it's all a lie
Frail is the cell
Against the immortal wound
Forcing a slow march
To a cadence of doom

p.s. I know it's a little morbid,
But when fate rubs your nose in your
Mortality you tend to have these
Thoughts

Hello

Written: February 8, 2019

"Hello are you there?"
I'm here
Lost
Somewhere between life and death
If there's a heaven
As there's an Earth
Let me find it
If there's love to be had
Let me have it
Love, the glue that holds
The space between the here and now
If you build a bridge
Let me cross it
On the other side they say
The grass is always greener
If I'm blind let me see
Remove the vail
Open my eyes to the light
Let the sun warm me
Let the breeze cool me
Let the rain quench my thirst
Let the night rest me
Let the garden calm me

CHARLES WAYNE CUMBIE

Let the gentle hand soothe me
Let God call out my name
I'll follow the sound 'till I'm home
"Hello are you there?"
I'm here
Lost
Somewhere between life and death

POEMED | RELIGION

The Caeser Coin

Written: July 31, 2018

When the choice to be made lies in the realm of the shady grey the yes or no of the coin will show the lack of what we need to know.

Yes or no the Caesar coin points the way decides your day, thumbs up thumbs down tomorrow or no tomorrow decisions made in sorrow.

You try to plan the winning game but life's not meant to stay the same the Caesar coin will call your name and decide your fate with no one to blame.

In coin speak you are or you ain't, only one of two sides can be given. The Caesar coin decides if you go or if you stay with the living.

So, flip the coin, choose your side. Are you team dying or team living or maybe team forever if you're dreaming.

May you find your Caesar coin, and may it still have some good luck showing so, toss the coin and seal your fate and hope that for you, you're not too late.

p.s. My Caesar coin is 139 years old, it's much older and wiser than me and, of course at the finish of the poem I had to toss the Caesar coin, just to see. Sorry to say, it was tails for the dying. But hey, I'm no gloomy Sunday, I kept trying. I went for two out of three and came up living. Hurray! For team living.

This is my 'Caesar' coin:

Bury your Dead

Written: November 19, 2018

The dead are best served cold to their bed
The same could be said of bad memories
They're best served old to their bed
Let go of them
Bury your dead
Forget the wrongs and ills of life
So much brighter it will be
When the blinders are shed
Bury your dead
When the weight of the world makes your worries unfurl
Wrap them in a bow and put them to bed
Bury your dead
Turn your gaze from the carcass decayed
Of memories gone bad
Bury your dead
When you're depressed take a recess
From those tired sad old memories
Go ahead
Bury your dead
Raise the dark shades and let the light in
Let a new day begin
Give up the dread
Bury your dead

CHARLES WAYNE CUMBIE

A Stranger's Pen

Written: November 9, 2018

When I look back on all the poems I've written, it seems so strange, like a stranger's hand held the pen. I find myself, the poet, a stranger to my own words therein. As I sat with my granddaughter one evening, we shared the words of my poems together--what a happy, happy feeling as we laughed together at the funny puns and silly thoughts that this stranger's hand had rendered. Though the pen set to paper may not be remembered, and the thoughts there no longer linger, the stranger's hand that held the pen I know was no stranger, he was a friend.

p.s. This poem was inspired by Maddy my granddaughter Who found that one of my poems "fast food" could make her laugh

Sounds

Written: March 23, 2019

Give me sound
Let the worship begin, let the Holy Angels in.
Give me sound
That rhythm, rhythm that shakes you to the ground.
Give me sound
Let me hear those guitar strings sing a melody of spring. Let me hear them, let me dream.
Give me sound
Maybe a whistle on the gentle wind let my heart beat feel relaxed again.
Give me sound
And life will be the thing we've found as we spin round and round.
Give me sound
A cricket's serenade, a tree frog calling from the shade. Life will be the sound that's made.
Give me sound
The ocean waves, the call of seagulls as they fly. I'll touch the sand, smell the salty air and feel the breeze on my face and I will stay there's no rush to go away.
Give me sound
We will dance to the tune that's played. I'll love you and you'll love me all our nights and all our days we'll use up till there's nothing left to throw away.
Give me sound.

CHARLES WAYNE CUMBIE

Stories Told

Written: February 24, 2018

On words of the pages
Like the gospel of the sages
I've let you see into my soul

I've poemed a rhyme
Tried to make sense of time
I've let you see into my mind

With thoughts I've conveyed
I bring light to the shade
I've let you see of what I'm made

With a life of mistakes
And regrets I can't shake
I've learned to try harder each time

So I write the poems
And open up the doors and windows
To my heart and soul
And when my dust settles
All that will be left
Is the poemed stories I've told

ACKNOWLEDGEMENTS

I wish to give a thank you, a handshake, and a hug to my son, Mike, who put in a lot of typing time to make this book possible, thank you Mike so very, very much.

ABOUT THE AUTHOR

Charles Wayne Cumbie was born in North Carolina in 1950. Son, Brother, Husband, Father, and now Poet. Poetry was something he started later in life. *Poemed* is his first completed work, a collection of poems and short stories from 2010 to 2019.

www.ingramcontent.com/pod-product-compliance
Lightning Source LLC
Chambersburg PA
CBHW052013070526
44584CB00016B/1728